DAVID CRONENBERG'S
A HISTORY OF VIOLENCE

C000075821

Arguably the most famous and critically acclaimed Canadian filmmaker, David Cronenberg is celebrated equally for his early genre films, such as *Scanners* (1981) and *The Fly* (1986), and his dark artistic vision in films such as *Dead Ringers* (1988) and *Crash* (1996). The 2005 film *A History of Violence* was a mainstream success that marked Cronenberg's return to the commercial fold of Hollywood after years of independent art house filmmaking. His international reputation grew and his work was honoured with numerous awards and two Oscar nominations. *David Cronenberg's 'A History of Violence'* – the lead title in the new Canadian Cinema series – presents readers with a lively study of some of the filmmaker's favourite themes: violence, concealment, transformation, sex, and guilt.

Bart Beaty introduces us to Cronenberg's film, situating it in the context of its aesthetic influences, and argues for its uniquely English-Canadian qualities. The author contends that *A History of Violence* is a nuanced study of masquerade and disguise, a film that thwarts our expectations of film genre as much as it challenges our perception of national geography and cultural mythology. As a contribution to the Canadian Cinema series, the volume also presents readers with an overview of Cronenberg's career, the production history of the film, and a discussion of its critical reception.

David Cronenberg's 'A History of Violence' is a book for fans, critics, and cinephiles alike.

(Canadian Cinema)

BART BEATY is an associate professor in the Faculty of Communication and Culture at the University of Calgary.

CANADIAN CINEMA 1

DAVID CRONENBERG'S

A HISTORY OF VIOLENCE

BART BEATY

UNIVERSITY OF TORONTO PRESS
Toronto Buffalo London

© University of Toronto Press Incorporated 2008
Toronto Buffalo London
www.utppublishing.com
Printed in Canada

ISBN: 978-0-8020-9932-7 (cloth)
ISBN: 978-0-8020-9622-7 (paper)

Printed on acid-free paper

Library and Archives Canada Cataloguing in Publication

Beaty, Bart
David Cronenberg's A history of violence / Bart Beaty.

(Canadian cinema ; 1)
Includes bibliographical references.
ISBN 978-0-8020-9932-7 (bound)   ISBN 978-0-8020-9622-7 (pbk.)

1. Cronenberg, David – Criticism and interpretation.   2. History of
violence (Motion picture).   I. Title.   II. Series: Canadian cinema
(Toronto, Ont.) ; 1

PN1997.2.H573B42 2008   791.4302'33092   C2008-905192-0

University of Toronto Press acknowledges the financial assistance to its
publishing program of the Canada Council for the Arts and the Ontario Arts
Council.

University of Toronto Press acknowledges the financial support of its
publishing activities of the Government of Canada through the Book
Publishing Industry Development Program (BPIDP).

Contents

DAVID CRONENBERG'S
A HISTORY OF VIOLENCE

Introduction

INTERVIEWER: But the feeling isn't one of being an outsider surely, because you know you're not an outsider anymore.
DAVID CRONENBERG: Well, I don't agree. I am. I'm just much more in disguise.[1]

The turning point in *A History of Violence* occurs when the Philadelphia-born mob killer finally drops the disguise of small-town Indiana family man. Even up to the very moment before, the film has retained a certain ambiguity about the real face of Tom Stall, the lead character played by Viggo Mortensen. Standing on the porch of his farmhouse, shotgun in hand and wife by his side, Tom holds his head high, his face open and untroubled by lines of worry. He is a righteous man, defending his home in true American fashion. His voice betrays no sign of nerves when he looks into the eyes of the men who have come to kill him as he tells them, 'Get off our property.' Yet when these same killers confront him with an unthinkable choice – his life in exchange for that of his son – he is a man transformed. Tom, his back to the camera, restrains his wife, quietly yet definitively asserting his dominance. 'I will get him,' he assures her, and he orders her into the house to care for their infant daughter. Because his face is hidden from the camera by Edie (Maria Bello), we do not see, Hulk-like, the transformation of this man. Nonetheless, when he turns once more to face the camera, Mortensen is no longer Tom. A different man, Joey Cusack, stands before us. His head now canted slightly towards the ground, brow suddenly furrowed, a cold and merciless glint in his eye, he speaks to his son in a voice and an accent that are alien: 'Go back to the house, Jack.' As he walks past the man he has known as his father, Jack gapes uncomprehending. He spins for a second look as he passes, knowing that the man before him is not the man who raised him. The disguise is dropped, and an outsider is revealed in the midst of this all-American family.

The resurrection of Joey Cusack in the gunfight at the old Stall place is a moment that transforms not only this man and his family, but a filmmaker as well. David Cronenberg, who made his name crafting a cinema of outsiders, visionaries, lunatics, and criminals, has returned to work for a Hollywood studio for the first time in nearly two decades. With this film, he re-established himself as one of the most important directors of his generation. Concluding a long series of critically adored box office disasters, *A History of Violence* moved Cronenberg once again into the centre of contemporary film culture. The film was almost universally praised. *The Village Voice*'s annual poll of film critics named it Best Picture of 2005, according it the greatest margin of victory in the history of the balloting. He joined a long list of cutting-edge Hollywood filmmakers who had previously claimed this distinction, including Spike Jonze (*Being John Malkovich*), David Lynch (*Mulholland Drive*), Todd Haynes (*Far From Heaven*), Sophia Coppola (*Lost in Translation*), and Richard Linklater (*Before Sunset*). With the exception of Lynch, each of these previous winners represented a generation that came of age in the wake of Cronenberg's influence. His triumphant return to glory seemed to signal the revival of a once major talent. In the same poll, Cronenberg himself was named Best Director, with a total vote rivalling that of the second- and third-place finishers, Wong Kar-wai and Jia Zhangke, combined. The filmmaker's critical success was not, of course,

1.1. Tom is transformed into Joey. ©MMV, New Line Productions, Inc.
All rights reserved. Photo by Takashi Seida. Photo appears courtesy of
New Line Productions, Inc.

entirely unprecedented. His previous two films, though little seen by the multiplex public, had also earned spots on the *Voice*'s poll (*eXistenZ* [1999] in 26th place, and *Spider* [2002] at 73rd), and critic J. Hoberman noted that, as far back as the 1970s, no director had been as consistently well reviewed by the *Voice* as Cronenberg.[2] Nonetheless, *A History of Violence* marked a particular return to both critical and commercial favour, a rebirth for a filmmaker who had struggled to find an audience for a series of highly personal films. In taking on a work-for-hire project, in disguising himself as an insider in the Hollywood system, Cronenberg found the film that would place him, once again, at the centre of contemporary cinema.

In an industry in which timing is everything, *A History of Violence* certainly benefited from the circumstances surrounding its release. Debuting in September 2005, the film emerged at a moment in which many Americans found themselves questioning both the myth and the reality of their nation. Opening on the same weekend as Thomas Vinterberg's starkly anti-American art film *Dear Wendy*, *A History of Violence* found favour among critics who recognized it as a sympathetic and mildly troubling commentary on contemporary America, what the *New York Times*'s Manohla Dargis called 'the feel-good, feel-bad movie of the year.'[3] Seemingly stalemated in an increasingly unpopular war, a conflict that itself had been launched on completely fabricated pretences, the United States had reached, if not a crisis of faith in itself, at least a period of contemplation. A well-crafted thriller so clearly enunciating these self-doubts was warmly received by critics longing for more substance than could be found in the fall's other major releases, *King Kong* and *Sin City*. The *Washington Post*'s Desson Thomson avowed that the film was 'a sobering reflection on our culture's attitude toward violence,'[4] and Kenneth Turan wrote that *A History of Violence* was 'a ticking time bomb of a movie, a gripping, incendiary, casually subversive piece of work that marries pulp watchability with larger concerns without skipping a beat.'[5]

But what, specifically, were the larger concerns that Turan and other critics identified? The heart of *A History of Violence*, many critics contend, is its subversive quality, the film's desire to have its cake but eat it too. J. Hoberman wrote that the film impersonated 'an action flick in its staccato mayhem while questioning these violent attractions every step of the way.'[6] It is commonly argued about the film that this questioning stems from Cronenberg's tendency throughout to cut to the consequences of the violent acts, to highlight the horribly mutilated faces and bodies of the victims of the violence that traditional action films elide. Thus, according to Rene Rodriguez, Cronenberg's careful close-ups of wounds 'force you to consider what it means, exactly, to shoot someone in the face, and how once that line is crossed, it becomes much easier to do it again.'[7] For many critics, the beauty of *A History of Violence* is the way that it expertly stokes in its audience a desire to see violence explode on screen, but then necessitates a kind of moral accounting for that desire, extracting a toll in the form of a critical self-awareness of the fact that such a desire carries significant consequences. Following this logic, the strength of *A History of Violence* is its ability to create a sense of shame in the audience, to provoke a visceral response that itself is immediately condemned as regressive. As Scott Foundas indicates in *LA Weekly*, Cronenberg 'holds up a mirror, but he leaves it up to us to recoil at what we see.'[8]

Yet the question that necessarily follows is what are the consequences of Cronenberg's consequences? Rene Rodriguez goes so far as to suggest, '*A History of Violence* illustrates how easily we accept violence as a way of defending our norm when it is threatened, which has led some viewers to interpret the movie as a critique of U.S. foreign policy (a reading Cronenberg has not discouraged in interviews).'[9] While this interpretation accords nicely with an American nation exhausted from the post-9/11 geopolitical failures of the Bush administration, despite Rodriguez's assertion, it sits uneasily with Cronenberg's statements.

Indeed, it is fair to ask whether the film is actually a critique of violence, let alone American foreign policy. It might seem uncharitable to suggest that many perceptive critics have got the meaning of this film so wrong, but in many cases Cronenberg and the critics do appear to be speaking at cross purposes. If we take his statements to the press at face value, a rather daunting 'if' when we are dealing with a film about deception, it would seem that *A History of Violence* is not a critique of American power at all.

In the press kit for the film, Cronenberg suggests that all the violence that Tom commits is justifiable.

> So the Tom Stall character is forced into violence when there was really not much of an alternative for him. At the same time, we don't cover up the fact that the violence that he commits now has very nasty consequences for the people who are the subject of the violence. I think you come away with thinking that violence is an unfortunate but very real and unavoidable part of human existence. And we don't turn away from it, and you can't really say that it's never justified. You can say that it's never very attractive, though, and that is the approach we've taken.[10]

Cronenberg's sense that the violent acts committed by his character are merely unfortunate and unpleasant is a far cry from the condemnation of those acts – or, indeed, of larger real-world acts of violence – that his critics find in the film. If we follow the director's logic, it is difficult to accord a critical or subversive sensibility to *A History of Violence*, and the celebratory tone adopted by many reviewers begins to crumble. David Edelstein, writing in *Slate*, was one of the few critics not swayed by claims about the film's subversive nature. While he acknowledges that the film is 'an absolutely sensational piece of filmmaking,' he rejects the suggestion that it is a critical work, offering that 'the movie belongs to a hallowed but problematic genre: guilty pulp. Here, you have your cake but choke on it, too.'[11] For Edelstein, the film's purported politics, a facile façade of criticism with no teeth behind it, might be just the sort of high irony that gets critics shouting, 'Masterpiece!' but he argues that on closer inspection the political and ethical position is revealed as hollow.

A scathing critique of middle America from David Cronenberg is not something that many filmgoers would readily anticipate. Academic critics have long been troubled by Cronenberg's status as a deeply conservative filmmaker. William Beard, a strong defender of Cronenberg, notes simply, 'his subject matter and his treatment are anything but "progressive."'[12] Other critics are more specific in their grievances, many of which are rooted in the director's treatment of gender. Thus, Claudia Springer, writing on *Crash* (1996), argues that the film 'does not introduce a radically altered form of sexuality. Instead, it perpetuates the continual filmic recycling of familiar misogynistic imagery.'[13] Christine Ramsay, discussing the same film, notes that Cronenberg's work shares 'a neo-conservative agenda concomitant with the crisis of straight white masculinity.'[14] Writing in the first book-length study of Cronenberg's career, *The Shape of Rage* (1983), critic Robin Wood extends the argument regarding the director's reactionary take on sexuality, suggesting that the filmmaker's entire world view is cynical and dystopian and offers an exceptionally negative view of humanity's capacity for change and improvement. He argues: 'if Cronenberg's films are reactionary, they are so in a quite unusual way ... When what we call normality appears in the films, it is presented as unattractive and joyless.'[15] Of course, this is a criticism that may have little bearing on a film like *A History of Violence*, in which middle-class normality might be troubled by the past and is possibly irreparably ruptured by knowledge in the present, but where that middle-class midwestern American lifestyle is nonetheless privileged as a kind of joyous Eden.

Cronenberg himself has been quite clear in interviews that despite the sometimes troubling sexualized visions he presents in his work, he is not opposed to middle-class values. Speaking to Chris Rodley, he describes his ambivalence about the middle-class lifestyle: 'I'm not prepared to totally throw out middle-class America. There are some things that are very valuable in the middle-class. I'm not a revolutionary in the sense that I believe that everything should be dismantled, destroyed and torn down and we must start from scratch. If that makes me a reactionary, then I plead guilty.'[16] More than any other film in Cronenberg's oeuvre, *A History of Violence* lays out this ambivalence in full view. A family drama, at least in part, the film shifts the director's focus from the individual in transformation, the subject of so many of his films, to the family in a moment of crisis. Because the United States, more than many societies, so thoroughly equates family and nation, it is understandable that many American critics are quick to see a film about the former as a statement about the latter. And, of course, despite what Cronenberg claims, *A History of Violence* is very much a film about American national culture. Yet at the same time, as close attention to its details reveals, it is about a great deal more than contemporary geopolitics.

If the politics of *A History of Violence* are, at best, muddy, the same can be said of its form and genre construction. Writing in the *Chicago Tribune*, Allison Benedikt calls the film 'really meta' because of the way that it is 'part action, part thriller, part Western, part comedy, part horror, part family drama.'[17] To which, of course, one could add several other categories that are just as prominent within the work. As Kenneth Turan notes, 'A History of Violence changes narrative direction and focus frequently without ever losing sight of the ideas behind its breakneck plot.'[18] Indeed, the near constant transformation of genre is key to the structure of the film, not merely as a showy form of postmodern Tarantino-esque meta-commentary on our image-saturated society, but as a reflection of the film's larger themes of deception, misdirection, and masquerade. In the simplest terms, the core of this film is the fact that it is a story about a man masking his true identity, in which the film itself introduces and then abandons dozens of generic constraints, one after the other after the other: the serial-killer/drifter film, the family drama, the bully film, the wrong-man film, the superhero-style action thriller, the gangster film, the film noir, the ironic gangster film, the 'smart' film, the Cronenberg film, and even the Canadian film. The question asked by the plot is 'who, really, is Tom Stall?' The question asked by the film is 'what, really, is this film?'

In the end, there are no easy answers to either of these questions. Does Tom remain Joey, or has Joey grown to be Tom in the process of becoming a husband and father? These are the questions that his family is left with at the film's conclusion, and that the audience is left to resolve to their own satisfaction. Is the film a genre work, a commentary on genre work, or a trans-generic hybrid? Is it all of these or none of them? And why is it so challenging, but ultimately so important, for critics to come to terms with the reality of this piece?

One reason for the confusion likely derives from the fact of the Cronenberg brand. Since he has produced, over the course of nearly forty years as a feature filmmaker, one of the most distinctive and idiosyncratic bodies of work in contemporary cinema, A History of Violence seems, on the surface, to be a radical break from the past. This is not the Cronenberg that we have come to know from his earlier work. Where in this film are Marilyn Chambers's phallically retractable armpit spike, James Woods's vaginal stomach opening, Jeff Goldblum's cabinet of bodily curiosities, and Jude Law's tooth gun? Where are the trademark 'Cronenbergian' moments of corporeal dread and revulsion? Knowing what we know about the director and his tendencies, it is difficult to watch A History of Violence without anticipating the arrival of such spectacles. But, of course, we wait in vain. Cronenberg, playing in his most realist style and to his most commercial audience in at least two decades, never quite delivers the horrors that we have come to expect of him. In the end, we are left with a film in which a maker of some of the most grotesque films in history suppresses the grotesqueries of the plot in order to tell the story about a man who is suppressing his true (and rather grotesque) nature. It is striking that, in playing to middle America, Cronenberg hides his true self in a film about a man hiding his true self in the middle of America.

One of the great challenges in writing about *A History of Violence* is the fact that disguises play such a central role. Tom is not what he first appears to be. Generically, the film is not what it first appears to be. I would add that neither is the promotion of the film to journalists and movie audiences what it appears to be. The very foundation of *A History of Violence* is a network of lies, and it behooves us to approach the film with the understanding that the filmmakers themselves seem to want to misdirect their audience. Nothing here is what it seems, and all evidence points to the fact that the filmmakers are playing games when they talk about the movie. The concept of masquerade, of pretending to be something that one is not, has a long and close affinity with film-making, precisely because actors put on roles. Yet in *A History of Violence*, I would suggest, it is also Cronenberg who is playing a role: the Holly-wood filmmaker.

Why, some will ask, include an American-financed work-for-hire film in a series dedicated to the exploration of Canadian cinema? Why write about a film that is so doggedly American in its subject matter and viewpoint? Obviously, Cronenberg himself is a director who is widely regarded as almost quintessentially Canadian. Indeed, a considerable body of scholarship and criticism has been dedicated to the project of highlighting the filmmaker's peculiarly and distinctly Canadian attributes and dispositions. William Beard, arguably the most significant of Cronenberg's interpreters, has suggested that Cronenberg has '"Canadian" characteristics,'[19] which prominently include the rejection of – or exclusion from – the dominant American model of the heroic male lead. Beard argues that passivity, weakness, and ineffectiveness tend to characterize Cronenberg's male leads, particularly in his earliest films. He is emphatic that Cronenberg rejects 'the heroic male mythology of Hollywood narrative.'[20] But this is an observation that does not hold much water where *A History of Violence* is concerned. Joey is a spectacularly active, strong, and effective anti-hero, and even his alter ego, Tom, is a classically stoic American patriarch. Does the use of this masculine mythology, therefore, trouble what we know of Cronenberg's auteurist and nationalist sensibilities? Or is there something else altogether going on? Can one make the claim that there is an ironic distance from the American mythology evident in *A History of Violence*, a distance that has led some critics to view the film as a deconstruction of the particularly American attitudes that the film seems to endorse?

As we move towards an answer to these questions, it might be worth bearing in mind a comment made by actor William Hurt to Brian D. Johnson of *Maclean's*. Johnson recounts the conversation:

> Last month, at a film festival party celebrating the movie's Toronto premiere, I found myself locked in a conversation with a rather manic William Hurt, one of its stars. Bemoaning America's political and moral climate, he said he was afraid the title wouldn't play in the U.S.
> 'It's Latin-ated,' he said. 'It's une histoire de violence, a story of violence.'
> This was a bit abstruse. What's not to get?
> 'You get it because you're Canadian. In America, they won't get it.'[21]

Hurt's suggestion that even the film's title is in disguise – moreover, that it is a disguise that is apparent to Canadians while remaining opaque to American viewers – further heightens the centrality of masquerade in the interpretation of this film as both a piece of nationalist cinema and an apparent critique of a different national culture. Hurt's contention that Canadians 'get' *A History of Violence*, and perhaps, 'get'

David Cronenberg, speaks to what I see as the film's most important contribution to Canadian cinema: the way that it allows us, through its ironizing of American film genres, to come to terms with a model of Canadian spectatorship of American cinema. At the same time, however, Hurt's reading of the title seems inapt. *A History of Violence* is not a story of violence at all, but many stories of many forms of violence. And one of those stories, perhaps the most important of them, is a Canadian story about the violence that we seek to displace onto our American neighbours.

A History

[A History of Violence is] a kind of an inside-out version of what I normally do.

David Cronenberg[1]

David Cronenberg was sixty-one years old when he directed *A History of Violence*. The veteran of seventeen feature films in a career spanning nearly four decades, if he was not entirely a household name akin to Spielberg or Scorsese, he was, nonetheless, a distinctive and well-regarded directorial brand with a truly personal style. The term 'Cronenbergian' had come to define a certain type of cerebral visual horror, a style of bodily grotesque that extended well beyond the simple grossouts provided by lesser filmmakers. A winner of prizes from the Berlin and Cannes film festivals, an unprecedented five-time Genie Award winner for Best Director, he is arguably Canada's most celebrated living filmmaker. As early as 1983 critic Robin Wood called him 'the one authentic auteur of English-speaking Canadian cinema,'[2] and while that club has surely swelled over the ensuing decades, there can be little doubt that Cronenberg remains at the top of English Canada's cinematic class.

Few filmmakers have developed oeuvres that are so markedly singular in terms of a personal vision, yet at the same time so disparate in terms of generic interests. While he is characterized primarily as a hor-

2.1. David Cronenberg directs Viggo Mortensen. ©MMV, New Line Productions, Inc. All rights reserved. Photo by Takashi Seida. Photo appears courtesy of New Line Productions, Inc.

ror director, that term seems trivializing when the breadth of the director's interests are considered. Indeed, very few filmmakers have so thoroughly blurred the boundary between the art film and the genre movie. Cronenberg's first features, *Stereo* (1969) and *Crimes of the Future* (1970), were highly abstracted art films (the former was shown at the Museum of Modern Art), but they were most decidedly not the types of work to which audiences flocked. In an effort to pay his bills, in the early 1970s Cronenberg followed the lead of filmmakers such as George Romero and Tobe Hooper, making low-budget features in the horror genre, including psycho-sexual gore-fests such as *Shivers* (1975), *Rabid* (1976), and *The Brood* (1979). The tax shelter boom of the late 1970s allowed a director with a track record to find work on films with increasingly expansive budgets, and Cronenberg experimented in new genres, including the racing film *Fast Company* (1979) and science-fiction pictures *Scanners* (1980) and *Videodrome* (1982). With eight Canadian-made low- and mid-budget films under his belt in just over a decade, Cronenberg was among the most prolific of English-Canadian filmmakers and, based on the success of *Scanners*, one of the most marketable. He became known as a director who made smart, subversive films out of schlock-horror material. Such was his relative fame that he was chosen as the subject of the first book released by the Academy of Canadian Cinema. After his eighth feature film Cronenberg made the transition to Hollywood.

Working with producer Dino De Laurentiis, horror-master Cronenberg was chosen to adapt Stephen King's novel *The Dead Zone* (1983) to the screen. Provided with a $10 million budget and filming in his native Canada, which stood in for New England, Cronenberg crafted a hit out of one of the three King-inspired movies released that year (*Cujo* and *Christine* being the others); it earned more than $20 million in box office receipts. The success of the film opened new opportunities for him, and he was offered the chance to helm big-budget commercial movies such as *Flashdance*, *Top Gun*, *Witness*, and *Beverly Hills Cop*, none of which seem particularly Cronenbergian in retrospect. After a year spent working on an eventually aborted screenplay for the movie that would later become the Arnold Schwarzenegger blockbuster *Total Recall*, he found a new project that would take him further into the mainstream of the Hollywood film culture. Cronenberg's remake of *The Fly* (1986) for American studio Twentieth Century Fox was the biggest commercial success of his career. The film, starring Jeff Goldblum as a scientist accidentally transformed into a fly, grossed more than $60 million worldwide and opened up for the filmmaker the seemingly unlimited possibilities offered by Hollywood.

Having worked on successive adaptations and from screenplays that, uncharacteristically, were not fully his own, on his next project Cronenberg risked his hard-won commercial credibility on a more personal film, *Dead Ringers* (1988). The movie, starring Jeremy Irons as twin gynecologists, evinced the now familiar Cronenbergian tone with its focus on bodily abnormalities and hidden horrors. Nonetheless, it was not a project with the easy commercial hook of *The Dead Zone* or *The Fly*, and it failed to catch fire at the box office. *Dead Ringers* was followed by a film even closer to the director's heart, an adaptation of William S. Burroughs's high-modernist literary masterpiece, *Naked Lunch* (1991). Largely non-narrative, the film began Cronenberg's march back towards his art film origins. *Naked Lunch* was a commercial failure, grossing less than $3 million. An epic adaptation of David Henry Hwang's award-winning play, *M. Butterfly* (1993), shot in Hungary, France, and China, struck many as an extreme change of pace for the director, and it was, as William Beard notes, the most mainstream realist of his films to date.[3] But the aesthetic change did nothing to alter his luck at the box office, and the film fared more poorly than even *Naked Lunch*.

Coming off a pair of financially disastrous big-budget flops, Cronenberg retreated to Canada and smaller films. In *Crash*, an adaptation of

J.G. Ballard's novel, which focused on sex and bodily injury, he returned to a number of classically Cronenbergian themes. Similarly, *eXistenZ*, with its funky 'what is reality?' science fiction tropes and penetrative organic gameplay, was seen by many as a synthesis of, and extrapolation from, the director's work in the 1970s. Nonetheless, despite the return to his thematic roots, Cronenberg was unable to stop his negative momentum with the movie-going public. Not only did both films fizzle at the box office, but *eXistenZ*, with an estimated budget of $31 million (Canadian), became one of the biggest bombs in the history of the Canadian film industry. His next independent project, the psychological study *Spider*, starring Ralph Fiennes, similarly failed to make a commercial dent in the North American box office, grossing less than $2 million, although it fared somewhat better overseas. Significantly, Cronenberg had personally produced his last two money-losing films, and on *Spider* he deferred his own salary to get the film made. These decisions placed the director in a precarious financial situation, opening the door for a project like *A History of Violence*.

By 2004 David Cronenberg was a director desperately in need of a hit. Nearly two decades had passed since his last big success, and none of his previous five films had found significantly large audiences. Despite the fact that critics and film festival audiences increasingly heralded his work, as a director he had seemingly parlayed himself out of the realm of commercial cinema. In an interview with *Canadian Business* conducted at the 2005 Cannes Film Festival, Cronenberg was blunt when asked why he had returned to the hired-gun style of filmmaking that had characterized his work in the early 1980s: 'I needed the money.'[4] That money would come from New Line, a division of the Time-Warner media empire, which was looking for someone to adapt a little-known comic book about a mob hitman hiding in plain sight from his former employers.

Producer J.C. Spink, who had read John Wagner and Vince Locke's graphic novel and with partner Chris Bender pitched the concept to the film studio, initiated the film version of *A History of Violence*. Best known at the time for having produced the American versions of *The Ring* and *The Ring 2*, remakes of the acclaimed Japanese horror film *Ringu*, Spink and Bender had a first-look deal with New Line, the producers of Peter Jackson's blockbuster *Lord of the Rings* trilogy. New Line was interested in the project. They secured the rights, committed $32 million to the film, and brought on board screenwriter Josh Olson and director Cronenberg, who was charged with making his most commercial film in almost twenty years. According to the movie's promotional website, Cronenberg understood that his assigned task was to 'elevate the material,'[5] or to lend his prestigious, though no longer commercial, hand to what otherwise might be a fairly simple-minded, comic-book-derived, crime thriller.

If New Line envisioned Cronenberg's elevating the comic book material, it is difficult to imagine that they saw a well-established pedigree in their screenwriter. Josh Olson got his start in moviemaking working in the art department on 1980s science fiction fare such as *The Masters of the Universe* (1987) and *Warlock* (1989). He later turned to writing, and two of his screenplays were produced as direct-to-video action movies, *Hitman's Run* (1999) and *Instinct to Kill* (2001). In 2002 he wrote and directed a direct-to-video science fiction thriller, *Infested*, in which insects eat their victims from the inside out. This film, indebted to Cronenberg's own early horror film *Shivers*, may have indicated to the producers a certain simpatico sensibility between writer and director. Together the two sat down to revise the screenplay, making certain alterations and developing the action in ways that would force it away from the source material.

Armed with a completed script, the filmmakers set out to find the actors who would bring life to the work. Central to the casting was the role of Tom Stall / Joey Cusack. Here Cronenberg opted for Viggo

Mortensen, an actor who was primarily known for his character parts until he took on the lead role of Aragorn in Peter Jackson's adaptation of the *Lord of the Rings*. The connections between that film series and *A History of Violence* were not altogether obvious, although there were certain similarities. New Line produced both, and, more important, each was a story in which a man of action initially hides his identity before revealing his true self to the world. Cronenberg explained that he was attracted to Mortensen for the role because he combined traits of both the leading man and the character actor, a type of actor that he prefers: 'First of all they tend not to be afraid because they're not trying to protect some image they see of themselves as traditional leading men, but also it gives them a much bigger palette to paint from because they have all kinds of edges. I need a kind of eccentricity that is more typical of a character actor than a leading man, and yet still has a leading man presence and charisma.[6] For the role of Tom, Cronenberg found in Mortensen an actor who could play big and small with equal skill.

Maria Bello, best known for her award-winning work on the American television series *ER*, plays Tom's wife, Edie. Since 2000 she had starred in a series of mid-range American films and had been nominated for a Golden Globe for her performance in *The Cooler*. It was that role that inspired Cronenberg to cast her in *A History of Violence*.

Maria was a real discovery for me. When I saw her in *The Cooler*, the movie showed what she could do in terms of subtlety, a kind of really vulnerable sexuality that was very real. I thought she could play this very complex, and yet at the same time, simple character, who is a small-town lawyer who embraces the energy, closeness and comfort of a small town with a lot of energy and enthusiasm – not brow-beaten by that but rather empowered by it. I thought she could bring all of those qualities to this character, who, as things unfold in the movie, undergoes some profound changes and discovers hidden aspects of herself.[7]

2.2. Viggo Mortensen as Tom/Joey and Maria Bello as Edie. ©MMV, New Line Productions, Inc. All rights reserved. Photo by Takashi Seida. Photo appears courtesy of New Line Productions, Inc.

For the roles of the two major mob figures in the film, Carl Fogarty and Richie Cusack, Cronenberg sought out highly acclaimed and award-winning actors with whom he had not previously worked. As Richard Corliss notes, 'a movie that suggests we are all actors, playing the roles we're cast in, is catnip to stars. ... They get to be naturalistic and ironic at the same time.'[8] For the roles of the mobsters, Cronenberg found actors ideally suited to walk the line between irony and naturalism. Ed Harris, a four-time Academy Award nominee, plays Carl Fogarty. 'Ed is someone I've admired for years,' Cronenberg reports in the press kit. 'I thought he had the toughness, the presence and the charisma to carry off this character. I wanted him to be very real, very intense.'[9] For his part, Harris claimed to be interested in working on a film with Cronenberg that seemed to be, at least on the surface, so different from the material that the director is normally associated with. 'I was kind of interested in why exactly David wanted to tell this story, a pretty simple story on a certain level. David said he was "really interested in people's reality, and what is real and what isn't. How people play roles, what that's all about." And he said "I just felt this story encompassed a certain dynamic of that."'[10]

For the small role of Richie Cusack, Cronenberg turned to Academy Award-winner William Hurt. Entering only at the end of the film, Richie is a showy role that could be played in any number of ways. According to Chris Bender, 'We didn't want to play into the cliché mob figure, but cast someone who could make the antagonist more complex. William Hurt brings something so different to playing a gangster, so untypical. His voice as an actor is so unusual, I call what he brings to his part "Hurtisms."'[11] For Cronenberg, the role of Richie, little more than a cameo, required an actor with the gravitas to be taken seriously at the end of the film's long journey. 'William unearthed some incredible subtleties and unexpected layers of meanings from the dialogue, which is exactly what I wanted. As with the Carl Fogarty role, it's a relatively small role in terms of screen time. But it's absolutely a critical role. It has to be compelling, convincing, charismatic, scary and profound. So I really needed an actor of great substance to play that role.'[10]

In all the major roles, with the exception of the Stall children, who were played by newcomers Ashton Holmes and Heidi Hayes, Cronenberg focused on finding actors with the right reputations to elevate the material from its pulpish roots. Making a psychologically serious crime film required a cast that would command the respect of critics and audiences alike. To that end, he was highly successful. Cumulatively, this award-winning cast served to signal the film's status as an important and thoughtful meditation on its themes, rather than a mere Hollywood thriller, and collectively members of the cast were recipients of several major prizes. William Hurt won acting awards from the Austin, the Los Angeles, and the New York Film Critics Associations and was nominated for the Oscar for Best Supporting Actor. Ed Harris won the award presented by the National Society of Film Critics. Maria Bello won acting awards from the Chicago and the Kansas City Film Critics and was nominated for a Golden Globe in the category of Best Actress in a Dramatic Motion Picture. These performances helped to focus critical and commercial attention on the film during the fall-winter awards season, and, more important, provided the film with the credibility that it required in order to naturalize many of its more fantastic elements of generic trickery. Indeed, the heart of the film's realism is derived as much from the performances of the cast as from the spare art direction, subdued cinematography, and contemplative score.

After an award-winning cast was assembled, the production moved to Toronto so that the filmmaker could work with his familiar crew in comfortable surroundings. As Cronenberg indicates, there are tremendous advantages to collaborating with the same group from project to project:

The advantages are that you can focus on the work and not on tempera-ment; you know your crew's strengths and weaknesses and have already figured out how to work around them; you have decided you like to work with each other, and that makes you happy to see everybody every day; you have a history together – not a violent one – and that gives you reference points so that you can work with great efficiency and subtlety; you have huge respect for one another because you have seen each other do good work under pressure; your crew as family grounds you and sup-ports you and that gives you confidence.[11]

His regular crew included director of photography Peter Sucschitzky, working on his seventh Cronenberg film; composer Howard Shore, in his eleventh collaboration with the director; editor Ronald Sanders, par-ticipating on his twelfth Cronenberg film; production designer Carol Spier, who had worked with Cronenberg since the 1970s; and costume designer Denise Cronenberg, the director's sister. Together, this crew recreated rural Indiana and the dirty streets of Philadelphia in Toronto and the surrounding Ontario towns of Millbrook, Tottenham, and Uxbridge. The film was shot over eleven weeks from September through November 2004, Canada once again taking its historic role as a stand-in for the United States, a legacy of the 1980 film policies and 'runaway productions.'

In the end, the film succeeded in almost every way that the cast and crew could have wanted, debuting to critical raves, award nominations, and healthy returns at the box office. It was that rarest of movies, a financially successful, serious genre film about big issues. *A History of Vio-lence*, made its world debut in May 2005 at the Cannes Film Festival, where it was screened in competition for the Palme d'Or. Although it did not receive that prize, which was taken by Jean-Pierre and Luc Dardenne's *L'Enfant*, the film was widely praised during the fortnight of the festival by international film critics, many of whom had picked it as the best film. In September the film made its North American debut at the Toronto International Film Festival (TIFF) and one week later was given a limited pre-release in fourteen theatres. It opened to wide distribution on 30 September, appearing on 1,340 screens in Canada and the United States. Receiving overwhelmingly positive notices, *A History of Violence* went on to earn a domestic box office gross of $31,504,633. When this figure was combined with an international gross of $28,809,237, the film totalled more than $60 million in receipts, making it the second-most financially successful film of Cronenberg's career and ending his lengthy string of box office disappointments.

That this studio-driven and least Cronenbergian of Cronenberg films would be the project to reconfirm the filmmaker's stature as an auteur is something that some critics find ironic. Nonetheless, Cronenberg's career has always been marked by a series of oppositions: genre-based pulp versus modernist art cinema; independent versus studio production; big budget versus low budget; adapted versus original screenplay; and – dare I say it? – Canadian versus American viewpoints. *A History of Violence* is not aberrational in the canon of Cronenberg's work; rather, it is a film that simply appears so on the surface. As a close reading of the film demonstrates, the initial scepticism that confounded and intrigued Ed Harris is resolved when one considers not the question of what the film has to say, but the ways that it chooses to say it.

In considering the way that *A History of Violence* plays with generic expectations in order to reinforce its central theme of masquerade, it is worth noting how the film seeks to negate one of its most obvious influences: the literary adaptation. Its screenplay based the graphic novel by John Wagner and Vince Locke, *A History of Violence* could be regarded as one of an increasingly long line of 'serious' films adapted from non-traditional, that is, non-superhero, comic book sources. This sub-genre of the comic-book-derived film, which includes recent films such as *Ghost World* (2001), *From Hell* (2001), *The Road to Perdition* (2002), and *American Splendor* (2003), laid a foundation for transforming the long-maligned comic book into a newly reputable source of inspiration for serious-themed and adult-targeted filmmaking in the 2000s.

Nonetheless, the relationship of this film to its source graphic novel is problematized by the fact that in numerous interviews Cronenberg has stressed that when he was hired on to the project by New Line, he was unaware of the fact that Josh Olson's script was based on a comic book. Speaking at the 2005 San Diego Comic Con International as part of the press junket promoting the fall release of *A History of Violence*, Cronenberg told the crowd of assembled comic book fans that he had been unaware that his film was an adaptation of a graphic novel until he was well into production. In an interview with Rebecca Murray conducted at that time, he notes:

> I never knew there was a graphic novel involved so it wasn't as though I approached this [as an adaptation]. It's not like when I made 'Naked Lunch' where it was, in a way, an homage to William Burroughs and his work. In this case I didn't know that there was a graphic novel so I had no attachment to it. No investment in it. And, really, my investment was in Josh [Olson]'s script. We had developed it to a certain point that it was going in a very interesting direction and we were both very comfortable with it, and that's when I heard that there was a graphic novel.' And I said, 'Well, what graphic novel? And they said, "Oh you didn't know?"'[12]

On a certain level the idea that a filmmaker of Cronenberg's stature could be unaware of the origins of his script seems to defy credulity, particularly given the significant ways in which in certain scenes, such as the initial shooting in the diner that brings Tom to the attention of the mob, the visual similarities between the comic book and the film are quite striking.

If we find credible Cronenberg's claim that he simply did not know about the source graphic novel, there are at least a few good reasons to believe him. Certainly, the filmmaker has never previously hidden the fact of adaptation in some of his other films. Indeed, Cronenberg has adapted for the screen many works from a number of genres with varying pedigrees, including four novels (Stephen King's *The Dead Zone* [1983], William S. Burroughs's *Naked Lunch* [1991], J.G. Ballard's *Crash* [1996], and Ian McGrath's *Spider* [2002]), a Tony Award-winning play (David Henry Hwang's *M. Butterfly* [1993]), and a 1950s B-Movie (*The Fly* [1986]). As Mark Browning has argued, 'there is a nexus of literary connections surrounding Cronenberg's films'[15]. Taking into account the director's openness to projects based on existing material and the heterogeneity of his source material, which ranges from cutting-edge modernist prose to the pulpy underbelly of popular culture, his denials could plausibly be taken at face value. In the past Cronenberg has never played the role of the auteur with something to hide, so why would he deny the truth about a graphic novel now?

Yet at the same time, something seems slightly off about this claim. Given the way that *A History of Violence* so relentlessly pursues the logic of masquerade, there would be a certain poetry involved for the filmmaker himself to misrepresent the roots of this project in his promotion of it. The question arises: would a scepticism about Cronenberg's claims shed additional light on the film itself? It is true, as he has repeatedly told interviewers, that significant differences exist between the two versions of the story. As he told Murray: 'So then I looked at it and I saw that although the basic premise was obviously the same, it then took some turns and went in a very different direction from what we were doing.'[14] To this end, before we embark on the process of unravelling the masquerade performed by this film in terms of its narrative and its production, it is worth considering the important ways that the film is both similar to and different from the comic book upon which it is based, particularly insofar as the changes between the versions will highlight the central concerns of the filmmakers. Significantly, the film itself makes little effort to be read as a comic-book-inspired film within the limits of its form, but, as Cronenberg's appearance at the San Diego Comic Con illustrates, it does raise that issue in both its production and its promotion.

On the one hand, it is easy to see a trip to San Diego as simply an insignificant stopover on the director's post-Cannes, pre-TIFF promotion of his upcoming film. Starting around 2000, San Diego has become more than a summertime comic book convention, transforming itself into the central locus for fans of all forms of 'geek culture.' As such, it has become such an important pilgrimage site for film and television producers pitching science fiction, fantasy, and comic-book-derived media properties that the convention itself has become the fodder of Hollywood-insider parody on HBO's *Entourage* and an important promotional destination for the likes of Cronenberg, a director whose history of exploding heads is sure to find a receptive audience for a new project based on a comic book.

As comic book culture has become increasingly mainstreamed by Hollywood since the mid-1990s, new opportunities have arisen for cross-media synthesis. From the perspective of the Hollywood studios, comic-book-derived movies have the advantage of arriving with a pre-sold audience of diehard fans who are likely to promote the film through word of mouth and guarantee a strong initial weekend at the box office. The ability of Hollywood to service decades of pent-up fan demand has resulted in a number of blockbuster franchises, including *Spider-Man* and *The X-Men*. Nonetheless, films based on more idiosyncratic or less known comics, such as *Ghost World* or *American Splendor*, have not particularly benefited from this blockbuster logic, instead positioning the art comic as akin to the contemporary art film or, more precisely, to what Jeffrey Sconce has termed 'the American smart film.'[15] Sconce's sense of the smart film as a Hollywood-produced, big-budget film designed to convey an independent cinema vibe through its reliance on irony and black humour aptly describes A History of Violence, which sought to capitalize on the newly won cultural capital accorded to independent comics even as the director distanced his project from its source.

Paradox Press, an imprint of DC Comics, originally published A History of Violence, the comic book written by John Wagner and illustrated by Vince Locke, in May 1997. Created in 1995, Paradox focused on the publication of non-superhero comic books targeted at traditional bookstore chains rather than comic book specialty shops. To this end, they specialized in short-story collections and long-form crime fiction, including A History of Violence and Max Allan Collins and Richard Piers Rainer's Road to Perdition (1998), itself the source of a critically successful film adaptation. Wagner, best known as the co-creator of the British action comic series Judge Dredd, and Locke, a journeyman artist working for DC Comics on a variety of projects, created a graphic novel in which the life of Michigan family man Tom McKenna is forever changed by the events that occur in his diner, which reveal his hidden violent past. At the time of its release the comic book was not widely reviewed, nor were its sales high enough to have warranted keeping it in print. The book was returned to circulation by another DC imprint, Vertigo Comics, only to coincide with the release of the film. It would be fair to say that, absent the film version of the story, the comic book would be little remembered, even by fans of crime comic books.

The comic book version of A History of Violence is divided into three chapters, each approximately 100 pages in length. Most of the story told in the film is contained in the first of these three chapters, which ends with the death of the mobsters that have come to kill Tom and his family. The second chapter, which is almost completely absent from the film version, tells the story of Tom/Joey's youth in Brooklyn, and provides details about his relationship to the mafia killers who want to see him dead. Like the third act of the film, the third chapter of the book finds Tom returning to deal with the mobsters who will continue to threaten his bucolic lifestyle, although there is almost no other similarity between the two concluding sequences. At the most basic level, the film performs a series of minor changes with regard to the source material. Some are largely inconsequential to the story, such as moving the action from Michigan and New York to Indiana and Philadelphia (a city that more closely physically resembles the film's shooting location, Toronto). Other changes, such as shifting the character names from Italian to Irish, serve both to trouble the generic expectations associated with films about the mafia and, with the name change from McKenna to Stall, to act as a subtle commentary on Tom's life under the mask of the nondescript family man. Nonetheless, these minor differences pale in comparison with the much more significant alterations to the story made by Cronenberg and screenwriter Josh Olson.

In the promotional material for the film, Cronenberg notes that the most important difference between the two versions of the story is the relative emphasis on the family and on the mafia. The graphic novel, he asserts, is far more interested than the film in 'mob stuff,' which places a greater emphasis on the relationships among the members of the Stall family. It is true that the film does make a large number of changes to the familial relationships and significantly reframes Tom's life in the small town. In both versions of the story, Tom is married to a woman named Edie. The film's Edie is a notable small-town career woman, a lawyer who presumably earns more than her diner-owning husband. As demonstrated by the scene in which she forces herself to cry so that Sheriff Carney will leave their house, she is sharply perceptive and has a keen understanding of interpersonal psychology. While she is taken aback by her husband's revelations from his hospital bed, she is portrayed throughout the film as every bit the equal of Tom. This is not the case in the graphic novel. The Edie McKenna of the original work is a housewife who has virtually no defined role beyond offering support to her husband. The breadth of the distinction between the two fictional wives can be seen in the reactions to Tom's revelation that he really is the man he has been accused of being. While the Edie of the film is stunned into a bout of violent nausea, the comic book Edie, when asked if she can forgive the man who has lied to her for more than twenty years, calmly replies, 'Of course I do, Tom. It's all been a ... a bit of a shock, that's all. You're still the man I married – the man I love.'[16] Crucially, the differing portrayals of Edie – conflicted yet intrigued in the film, placidly, even docilely, accepting in the novel – serve to highlight the important way that the film addresses broadly familial issues, while the book is far more concerned with the individual protagonist. Significantly, in the graphic novel Tom outlines his plans for eliminating the mob boss to both his wife and his son, who encourage him in this violent quest. With this, the book removes any hint of moral ambiguity around Tom's actions, as it eagerly endorses the killings through the vicarious involvement of his family.

This distinction is similarly played out with regard to the father-son relationship as it is established in the two texts. In Cronenberg's film, the relationship between Tom and Jack Stall is central to the construction of an argument about identity. Jack is an outsider in his school, a pot-smoking victim of bullying who is slowly ushered into a world of hyper-masculine violence through the actions of his father and, ultimately, through his own participation in the killing of Carl Fogarty. In the book, however, Tom's son is quite different. Buzz McKenna is not an outsider, but a popular student with a number of friends, who is dating 'the fantastically beautiful Laura Appleby.' While each version of the story brings the Fogarty-Tom showdown to a climax through the abduction of the son, in the book the son's only role is as a hostage. In the book, when Tom is defeated and held at gunpoint by Fogarty, it is not the son who steps forward with a shotgun to assume the patriarchal authority, but Edie who rescues her husband. In the comic book, Buzz is a thoroughly uncomplicated character, the good son convinced of his father's righteousness and supportive of his exploits. The film, on the other hand, provides a much darker image of father-son relations in which violence is part of a legacy ushered down from generation to generation, and the changes in these relationships made from the source text to the finished film highlight the centrality of the familial aspect of the text.

While Cronenberg's film has dramatically shifted the terrain of the family from the book, an even more important transformation has affected Tom's relationship with the mobsters who have come to kill him. For the most part, the distinction between the two texts is a function of the fact that the novel provides Tom's history in great detail, while the film hints at it only vaguely. Indeed, the entire second chapter of the book deals with Tom's history with the Manzi mob and with John Torrino, the disfigured mobster seeking a measure of vengeance. Richie is not Tom's brother, but a neighbourhood friend from Brooklyn, whose own brother, Steve, was a victim of the Manzi mob family. When Torrino, the Manzi's button man, murders Steve, Richie enlists the teenaged Tom in a plan to seek revenge on the Manzis by robbing their monthly payoffs and killing the entire mob family. In executing this plan, Richie is killed and Tom narrowly escapes with his life after a back-alley showdown in which he loses a finger to a cleaver-wielding Torrino and the mobster loses an eye to a stretch of barbed wire. Unlike the film, when Torrino reappears in Michigan he, like the reader, is unsure whether Tom is really the long-missing Joey, despite the fact that both are missing the same finger – a digit that Torrino wears around his neck in a glass vial as a reminder. It is only when Torrino sees Buzz, the spitting image of his father at a younger age, that he realizes the truth of Tom's identity and seeks his vengeance.

While the comic book provides greater clarity as to why Joey is being sought by these killers, it does so at the cost of a great deal of characterization. The ambiguity that surrounds Joey's background, particularly in his conversation with his brother Richie, heightens the film's drama by allowing the viewer to imagine the particularities of the backstory and plug the cipher-like Joey into a wide variety of generic narratives. Further, the lack of detail, coupled with Joey's amazing proficiency in combat, allows the viewer to imagine the protagonist as an even more vicious killer than is on view throughout the course of the film. Yet the opposite is true of the book. In Wagner and Locke's vision of Joey, he is a follower of the hotheaded Richie, a good boy lured into doing the wrong thing. Significantly, Joey is an orphan living with his impoverished but noble grandmother. Joey is not interested in helping Richie's plot against the Manzis until he learns that his ailing grandmother needs money for an operation. The opportunity to raid the Manzis stems not from a dark place in his own soul, but from misguided altruism. Indeed, when Tom reveals his murderous past to his wife and son and confesses his past crimes to the police, he anticipates only a suspended sentence for his share of a robbery that resulted in the murder of at least a half-dozen people, since, after all, his motives were pure and his victims were loathsome. Lest there be any misunderstanding, the Joey Muni of the graphic novel is a good boy who fell in with the wrong crowd, but who has since led an exemplary life as Tom McKenna, to which he will return, with the full support of his family, once he has dispatched the remaining mobsters. Joey Cusack, on the other hand, is a violent and shadowy figure who has caused untold problems for the Philadelphia mob, a force for evil as much as a force for good. The film significantly troubles the simple black and white moral logic of the comic book.

One of the most important structural changes wrought to the story by Olson and Cronenberg is the concluding act, which takes on a decidedly different shape because the filmmakers have made Joey and Richie brothers. Joey's trip to 'the City of Brotherly Love' to kill his sibling and end the threats to his family is central to the film's understanding of the way that violence is inherited and shared among family members. The conclusion of the comic book, on the other hand, is quite at odds with this motivation. In the third, and final, chapter of the book, Joey travels back to Brooklyn with his wife to confess to his youthful crimes. The key plot twist arrives with the realization that, after twenty years, Joey's friend Richie is not, in fact, dead, but is still a captive of the Manzi family. Thus, upon returning to New York, Joey gives his wife and the police the slip and confronts the Manzis in a warehouse in Brooklyn, where he kills a number of mobsters, including the new boss, Little Lou Manzi, and rescues his horribly mutilated friend Richie. Richie's survival is a difficult plot twist to swallow, even in the context of a comic book narrative, as it completely shatters any semblance of realism that the text might have established up to that point. The idea that a mob boss would trouble himself to keep his father's killer alive in a warehouse in order to repeatedly torture him for more than two decades defies all logic and serves little narrative function other than to reconfirm, through his mercy killing, the idea that Joey has not lost his soul.

In some ways, therefore, it is actually fair to suggest, as Cronenberg does, that his film is not based on the comic book. The narrative and thematic differences between the two works are so profound and thorough that, more than most adaptations, they truly do stand as distinct and isolable works. *A History of Violence*, as we shall see in the pages that follow, is not particularly interested in working through its differences with the graphic novel so much as it is in making connections to other films about the myth of America. Cronenberg's references in *A History of Violence* are not to the comic books of his youth, but to the cinema of the past. Throughout the film he veils its origins in the lowbrow pulp of the comic book industry, just as Tom Stall hides his Philadelphia origins with a midwestern accent. The masquerading undertaken by the film, and by Cronenberg himself as a director promoting his film to the public, can be seen as part of a much larger process of legitimization that is crucial to understanding the relationship between the source comic book and the film version of this story. Just as *A History of Violence* is, on the narrative level, a catalogue of various violent archetypes that it proceeds to hierarchize and problematize, so too, on the larger level of the film's position within a contemporary cinema culture, is it a work that comments on our preconceptions about genre, medium, and form. In the end, it is difficult to regard *A History of Violence* as merely a cross between a comic book film and a David Cronenberg film, despite the fact that the graphic novel, like the director, wears the mask of American middle-class domestic wholesomeness in order to obscure a violent and depraved past that it struggles mightily to conceal. There is a more complicated masquerade at work in this film, one that is almost entirely defined by the generic trajectories and bait-and-switch tactics of a director with something to hide.

Violence

We thought of the western – and yes, of course, how political do you want to get? The western myth of the homesteader with his gun, defending his family and piece of property against other men with guns. And does that become your foreign policy? All bets are off. The social contract is canceled. You are allowed to do anything in that situation. To that extent, when westerns are mentioned by the President as part of his foreign policy, when Osama bin Laden is wanted 'dead or alive,' you have to seriously think about the 'interbleeding' of genre, myth and realpolitik, which, I guess, is not that real.

David Cronenberg[1]

While promoting his new film, David Cronenberg was always quick to highlight the significant ways that *A History of Violence* draws upon generic conventions in order to problematize myths of America. For the most part, these conventions are almost purely cinematic, and from the film's very first shot the audience is invited to make connections between this work and the history of filmic violence. It is probably impossible to begin a movie with a single long take in this day and age without having the technique recall Orson Welles's classic 1958 late-era film noir, *Touch of Evil*. Certainly, Robert Altman, whose characters actually discussed the shot in a meta-textual fashion in the opening of *The Player* (1992), used the reference as a subtle signal that the Hollywood studio executives he portrayed were touched by certain forms of evil. So it seems just as likely that Cronenberg's four-minute and ten-second opening recalls Welles for a similar purpose. While Cronenberg's laconic horizontal tracking motion lacks the visual panache of Welles's cranes or Altman's eight-minute steady-cam virtuosity, the shot nonetheless serves the dual purpose of recalling Welles in a suggestive manner, but marking a level of distance at the same moment through the use of ironic humour.

Opening the discussion of a David Cronenberg film with attention to the way that it recalls its cinematic forebears may strike some readers as unusual. After all, Cronenberg, as Serge Grünberg succinctly notes, 'cannot be defined as a "cinephile" or a "movie brat."'[2] Indeed, few directors of his generation seem less immersed in the history of cinema. In stark contrast to a figure like Martin Scorsese, a colleague with whom he has frequently compared himself in interviews, Cronenberg's influences seem particularly anti-cinematic and personally idiosyncratic. Yet *A History of Violence*, produced as something of a break from his usual style, seemingly revels in cinematic referents. In watching the film it is difficult to imagine that one is merely watching an American story, because the film itself is awash in the traditions of American storytelling. Thus, while many critics might approach the film through the lens of Cronenberg's previous works, I have chosen to examine it for the way that it enunciates certain similarities to and differences from the traditions of American film genres that are primarily concerned with the issue of violence in society, a reading that is invited from the very opening scene. I want to suggest that *A History of Violence* is very much the film of a cinephile and, therefore, in some ways the least typical of all the director's projects to date. To demonstrate this, I have structured my analysis of the film not in a thematic manner, but chronologically. It is my goal to examine the ebb and flow of generic tropes as the film unfolds for its audience. However, I have exempted two scenes that cut right to the heart of the film's thematic concerns from the film's chronology so as to provide a more detailed comparative examination: the love scene between Edie and Tom and the later and much more violent sex scene between her and the man whom she now knows as Joey. This discussion appears at the end of the chapter.

A History of Violence opens with the high-pitched whine of insects, a piercing sound that places us instantly in a state of unease. With traffic noise in the distant background, the camera tracks from left to right across the face of a low-end rural motel. From the second door two men appear, the well-dressed Leland (Stephen McHattie) and his younger, T-shirt-wearing accomplice Billy (Greg Byrk). Billy casually straightens the lawn chair beside the door before heading to their blue convertible. Their gait marks their exhaustion and their dialogue confirms it. They are a picture of fatigued death, dragging themselves off to face another rootless, aimless, and disaffected day on the road. The measure of their alienation is expressed in the startling atmospheric shifts over the course of the opening sequence. 'Bring it on up to the office, I'm going to check us out,' Leland tells Billy. Paul Burch's 'Life of a Fool,' one of only two songs included on the soundtrack, plays on the car radio as Billy makes the slow, straight twenty-foot drive to the front office of the motel, where he turns off the ignition.

This short trip is the first of dozens of expectations that will be raised by the film only to be casually dashed, and it establishes in a clever and funny manner the basic logic of the narrative. If the laughter engendered by this pointless effort to drive twenty feet puts the audience momentarily at ease, that sense of comfort is quickly reinforced by a second light moment, when Billy asks Leland what took him so long to check out, despite the fact that he had been gone for less than thirty seconds. 'Nothing,' Leland replies, 'I had a little trouble with the maid, but everything's fine now.' But, of course, nothing is fine. When Billy enters the office in search of water we see the slaughtered bodies of the motel owner and, in a subsequent shot, the maid. If there is humour to be found here, it is the uneasy gallows humour of ruptured expectations. When a little girl in pigtails and a purple sweater emerges from a bathroom holding a doll, the scene no longer holds even a trace of lightness. Casually, reassuringly, Billy calms the girl as he pulls a revolver from the back of his jeans and calmly executes the young witness. Leland and Billy, it turns out, have not been merely touched by evil, but are positively awash in it.

This opening sequence serves a number of purposes in the film. First, it establishes the structuring tension between absurdly dark humour and horrifying violence around which the film revolves. More important, it establishes the fundamental evil that is Leland and Billy. Significantly, the wanton killing of the little girl creates for the viewer an impression that these men are entirely void of remorse or human feelings of any kind. They are established as perfectly horrific movie villains, the type that any decent cinematic action film hero would be wholly justified in killing. Third, the opening sequence quickly and succinctly establishes both the rules and the stakes for what will follow. Generically, audiences have come to expect that in a thriller the acts of violence will gradually grow in complexity and horror, each violent set piece serving to top the one before it. Starting from this logic, Leland and Billy are a particularly brutal ante in the stakes that will be the violence in this film.

Nonetheless, despite the fact that each of the three major acts of violence committed by Tom/Joey results in a greater loss of life than the previous one, *A History of Violence* is not merely about the escalation of violence. Indeed, the film is organized in a three-act structure, each act concluding with a scene of bloody fighting – showdowns with the serial killers in the diner, with Fogarty and his men at the Stall home, and with Richie and his men in Philadelphia. Each of these sequences wraps up what could conceivably have been a separate film. The diner sequence ends the movie about the drifter killers and the Stall family, but it opens the door for a classically Hitchcockian 'wrong-man' scenario. The shootout with Fogarty reveals the truth about Joey and eliminates the possibility of a wrong-man film, but it begins a more classically organized crime revenge film. Throughout the movie, narrative and generic expectations are established for the audience only to be quashed or resolved as the story veers off in a new direction. At the same time, other forms of violence – including non-lethal but potentially devastating psychological violence – weave through the story in a way that binds the film together thematically and keeps it narratively and tonally consistent even while it lurches from genre to genre. Indeed, A History of Violence does not rely merely on a series of cataclysmic set pieces, but builds from the premise that violence is fundamental to American middle-class life, and that it exists in every aspect of that life. From this perspective, Leland and Billy do not happen upon Tom Stall by chance, but are fated to do so simply because they are the purest expression of the violence that he has sought to repress for so long. Indeed, this point is driven home explicitly when Tom, arriving in the morning at his diner, cleans the garbage from the windowsill in front of his place of business, a process that precisely recalls the actions of Billy with the motel lawn chair, thereby visually equating the one killer with the other through their orderliness.

Yet the question to be asked from this equation is this: are Billy and Tom really equals in death? The film works relentlessly to question whether Tom's family can continue to love him after they see the true face of Joey, and although the ending is ambiguous on this question, there is at least the possibility of redemption. For Leland and Billy, on the other hand, no such hope exists. On his commentary for the DVD, Cronenberg recalls that actors McHattie and Byrk created an elaborate backstory for the killers as a guide to their own performances, but that history is elided in the film. Indeed, Leland and Billy have no history

3.1. Tom Stall arrives at his diner. ©MMV, New Line Productions, Inc. All rights reserved. Photo by Takashi Seida. Photo appears courtesy of New Line Productions, Inc.

that we are aware of – they exist only in the eternal present, a source of menace upon whom the viewer maps the histories of other serial killers. Cinematically, the affectless drifters contain echoes of prior road-based serial killers, a genre that was established in Richard Brooks's *In Cold Blood* (1967) with killers Perry Smith and Richard Hickock and refined with the portrayal of Kit Carruthers and Holly Stargis in Terrence Malick's *Badlands* (1973). These dramatizations of real-life killers emphasize the role of mutual reinforcement in the killings. Ineffective individually, as partners the killers enable sickening violence. That motif was reified by more contemporary fictionalized road killers, such as the hyper-mediatized Mickey and Mallory Knox in Oliver Stone's *Natural Born Killers* (1994) and the hopelessly mismatched losers-killers-for-hire, Carl Showalter and Gaear Grimsrud, in Ethan and Joel Coen's *Fargo* (1996). Whether played for maximum psychological realism or high irony, each of these killer pairs lends credence to an image of an underground of senseless and aimless American violence that targets not the urban metropolis, but the remotest parts of the American heartland. With no backstory of their own, save that of their cinematic forebears, the killers in *A History of Violence* head east, staying out of the big cities, straight into a collision with a man who has more than enough history for the three of them.

While the film might initially tease at an equivalence between Tom and Billy in their attention to neatness, the distinction between the Stall family and the killers who will disrupt their lives could hardly be more starkly drawn in the scene immediately following Leland and Billy's spree killing at the motel. A portentous nightmare awakens little Sarah Stall and brings her close-knit nuclear family running to her side. The scene not only introduces the main characters, including Tom Stall, but it also serves as the first indication of how wonderful life in the Stall household is. 'There were monsters,' Sarah tells her father. 'No, sweetie,' he assures her, 'There's no such thing as monsters.' Coming, as it does, immediately on the heels of Billy's cold-blooded execution of a girl no older than Sarah, it is easy to recognize the irony in Tom's words. This introduction of Tom as the reassuring and nurturing father figure stands diametrically opposed to the images of Leland and Billy that open the film, establishing a distance between the antagonists that the film's logic works very hard to narrow over the course of the story. While it is possible to read the cut-on-action from Billy's gun firing to Sarah's screaming as the girl awakening from a dream of the drifter killers, later events forcefully demonstrate the absolute reality of Leland and Billy. Nonetheless, the film does, at least initially, invite the viewer to consider the possibility that the opening is merely Sarah's dream, thereby establishing another narrative expectation, another mask, that is quickly undermined by the events of the story. The reality of the sequence serves as a reminder of how easily the American dream slips into the American nightmare, a theme that dominates much of the film.

Familial relationships permeate the scenes that follow, as Cronenberg quickly establishes the relations between the members of the Stall family, who gather in Sarah's room. Until the final scene of the film, Sarah will have only a minor role in the story except as a possible target of Fogarty's violence; she is little more than a pawn that the filmmaker places in danger to establish more complex narrative traps. The same cannot be said, however, about Tom's wife, Edie, and his son, Jack, each of whom takes on a central role in the course of the film. Jack Stall is introduced most fully at breakfast, in a scene in which a certain emotional distance from his father is established. While Jack kisses his mother upon entering the kitchen and is playful with his sister, he is subtly withdrawn from his father. He stops Tom from pouring his cereal, for example, assuring him that he can do it himself. Jack is a young man who is beginning to establish boundaries and claim his independence. In the process of defining his unique identity, however, it is clear that Jack suffers from low self-esteem. Noting that his class will play baseball in gym that day, Jack declares that he will have to 'suck hard in right field,' a statement that quickly establishes him as a non-athlete and therefore a likely outcast in small-town Indiana. When Tom offers his son some fatherly advice, Jack quickly corrects him, amending his observation and rebuffing his father's offer of support. The tension that exists in this scene between father and son is integral to establishing a new set of generic expectations in the audience. In these early scenes Cronenberg ably lays out the parameters of a small-town family drama, shifting the dramatic tension away from the Stall/ drifters relationship, which in any case has only been foreshadowed, and placing the dynamic within the family itself. We might expect, following the breakfast scene, that the central dynamic in the film will revolve around the relationship between Tom and Jack, and in some ways this is, in fact, the case. Certainly, we are prepared from this scene to anticipate the centrality of Jack's role in the film.

When we next see Jack he is standing, isolated, in right field. Cronenberg shoots the boy from a crane, emphasizing his loneliness as the patter of the baseball game plays in the background. Significantly, Jack is dressed in a bright yellow T-shirt with his school's crest on the breast, the colour a not-so-subtle signifier of the cowardliness he will soon demonstrate. When Bobby (Kyle Schmid), the domineering jock, strides to the plate, we are primed from his demeanour to recognize him as a classic teen-film bully. Bobby carries with him a certain set of expectations developed over dozens of movies in which a soft-spoken outsider is ruthlessly bullied by the local jock, ranging from the likes of *My Bodyguard* (1980), to *The Karate Kid* (1984), to *Spider-Man* (2002). When Jack's catch in right field robs Bobby of the opportunity to be the game-winning hero, the bully glares at him, brow furrowed and head slightly bent in a manner that foreshadows the menace that is revealed in Tom's transformation into Joey Cusack. Afterward, in the locker room,

Bobby and his mute sidekick (Morgan Kelly) confront Jack, accusing him of thinking highly of himself, of being 'the little hero' who 'saves the day at the last minute,' a role that Jack's father will soon assume. As Jack placates the bully by running himself down as a 'little, punk-ass, chicken-shit faggot bitch,' we become aware that this is a classic bully film formulation and that, because of the demands of the genre, it is inevitable that Jack will be called upon to defend himself physically. In this way, long before Carl Fogarty or Richie Cusack are posed as specific threats to Tom and, by extension, his family, Jack is established as the likeliest victim of violence in the film, and his story assumes centre stage, however briefly.

Yet *A History of Violence* is not simply a film about violence, or about its history, but more explicitly addresses certain hierarchies of violence. Specifically, the film deals with the way that particular forms of violence cut more deeply, affect pain more widely, than do others. By constantly shifting generic conventions and by establishing expectations that are then entirely brushed aside or minimized in favour of new threats, Cronenberg demonstrates that not all evils are created equal. This point is driven forcefully home the next time that we see Bobby and his friend as they cruise the main drag of Milford in their pick-up, determined to exact revenge on Jack. As Bobby brings the truck around towards Jack with the intention of kicking his ass, he accidentally cuts off Leland and Billy in their own pick-up truck. This beat-up old truck is something of a step down from the stylish blue convertible that the killers had been previously driving, and the change forces the viewer to momentarily reflect upon the various horrifying possible reasons for the switch in vehicles. Bobby, full of alcohol and the attitude of a teenager with fights to pick, quickly flips off the killers, who meet his gaze with eyes filled with bored, steely death. Chastened, Bobby and his friend retreat from the fight, clearing out as fast as the truck will carry them. With this interaction, the bully storyline is nearly abandoned, superseded by a far more dangerous threat than a scuffle between high school boys. A monstrous form of evil has rolled into town, and in the violence food chain Bobby and his friend are mere minnows confronted for the first time by sharks.

Less than three minutes pass from the time that Leland and Billy enter Stall's diner until they lie dead on the floor. The diner scene concludes the first act of the film in a riot of brutal violence, a fight that leaves two dead in the space of only seventeen seconds. It is an insignificant amount of screen time for an action that is so central to the narrative logic of the film, and it is freighted with import and seemingly slight but imperative moments. The scene opens with a short exchange re-establishing the diner as a community hang-out, where dating teens eat ice cream sundaes in a booth on the side wall and departing customers remind Tom that they'll see him in church. The arrival of Leland and Billy shatters this idyllic scene, the tone of their request for coffee and pie initially placing the locals on alert and their subsequent demand for the food causing alarm. Tom takes command of the situation, a peacemaker calmly reassuring the killers that their demands can be met in the same tones that he had earlier used to soothe his frightened daughter. It is clear from his demeanour and the deference he receives from his employees that Tom is the natural leader in this space, the man to whom the others turn for direction and, ultimately, salvation. Dismissing his waitress, Charlotte, for the night he begins to pour the coffee. Leland's quietly spoken 'Billy' raises Tom's eyes from the coffee mug and towards Charlotte. The part of him that is Joey knows precisely why Billy has been dispatched to the front door. In the counter shot, as Billy rises to intercept Charlotte, Leland, with hands folded in the foreground, looks up into Tom's eyes, the faintest smile tracing the outline of his mouth. This is a smile of recognition. Long before the audience has had a chance to see the dark recesses of Tom's soul, Leland discovers a kindred source of violence. Perhaps, in that surreptitiously exchanged

47

glance, he recognizes the man who, at last, will end his exhausting and deadly travels.

Significantly, and despite a number of important shifts in emphasis and tone, this scene, more than any other, recalls the action presented in the graphic novel. The catalyst of Tom's re-transformation into Joey, the scene largely plays as it was originally written. In both versions the sequence of major events in the fight is unchanged: Tom assaults the killers with the coffee pot before they can act; he vaults the countertop to retrieve the gun dropped by the scalded killer; and he uses that gun to blast the other man through the window. In the comic book, that shooting ends the violence. Tom places the gun on the other intruder, who surrenders rather than accepting his own death. In the film version, however, Leland continues the fight after Billy has been gunned down, drawing a knife from his sock and stabbing Tom in the foot. Tom retaliates by shooting Leland in the head at point-blank range.

Two other alterations to the scene as it plays in the comic book are important to understanding the construction of violence in the film. First, in the comic book, when the violence starts, Tom is alone with the killers in the diner. It is Tom, and Tom alone, who is menaced with violence. When he acts, he acts exclusively on his own behalf. Cronenberg's Tom, however, acts for Charlotte, the short-order cook Mick, the teenaged couple, and, indeed, for the kind of small-town society that is at the heart of American mythology. Cronenberg's film sexualizes the threat in the diner, situating Charlotte as the first victim ('Do her,' Leland yells at Billy) and generally ratcheting up the horror implicit in the scene. While little further work needed be done to render Leland and Billy deserving victims of cinematic justice after they so callously dispatched the family at the motel, Cronenberg does not let the opportunity to raise a genuine bloodlust in the audience pass. The violent exchange unfolds without dialogue, a second significant shift from the source material. John Wagner's original script is rife with clichéd dia-

3.2. Leland ignites the violence in the diner. ©MMV, New Line Productions, Inc. All rights reserved. Photo by Takashi Seida. Photo
appears courtesy of New Line Productions, Inc.

logue. As Tom swings the coffee pot he tells the killers 'you best have your coffee first!' As they regroup, the killers assure him that 'You're gonna die, scumsucker!' and call him a 'Stinkin' soda jerk!'[3] This purple prose adds little to the scene, except, perhaps, to position the killers squarely within the tradition of over-talkative comic book villains. Yet the absence of these none-too-witty threats from the film is important in creating some sense of realism within the scene, however delimited.

Generically, of course, the audience is primed for Tom's explosion of violence. Despite the fact that we have seen no evidence of a violent side to him, the intertextual presence of the valiant Aragorn, the generic expectation that good will triumph over evil in filmic moments such as this one, and the prior scene in which Tom is established as the stoic patriarch of an almost too perfect family assure us that Tom will emerge from this situation unscathed. Indeed, the foot injury that he sustains, like the velocity of the action and the lack of dialogue, comes across as nothing much more than a necessary nod towards realism. As Cronenberg explains in his DVD commentary: 'The idea in this sequence was to make Tom not be elegant and perfect in his disposal of the two bad guys, but awkward and nervous and worried and disturbed.' If this was his intention, he has seemingly failed. How else to describe Tom's actions – bounding over the countertop, spinning with the gun and dropping his target with precisely grouped shots – other than perfectly elegant? While Mortensen's Tom seems no different from any of a host of ordinary men turned killing machine by extraordinary circumstances (usually played by the likes of Arnold Schwarzenegger and Bruce Willis), his performance is far from awkward. While they don't yet recognize it, in his quiet mastery of events as they unfold, for the first time here the audience sees Joey, a figure seemingly recognized only by Leland.

Not only does the audience first meet Joey in this scene, they also unwittingly applaud the violent past that provided him with the skills to quickly dispatch the drifters. Again in the commentary, Cronenberg highlights the theme that he, like so many critics of the film, regards as central: the consequences of violence. 'The shot of Leland's face hanging there sets a pattern to come. That is to say that the violence here is exhilarating – the audience tends to applaud it – because after all it's set up to be completely justified. There is no question that those bad guys meant business and they opened themselves up to the violence visited on them. But at the same time I wanted the audience to see the results of the violence.' Cronenberg continues by noting that the scale of the violence in the film is intimate and, as in so much of his work, corporeal, a gruesome reminder of the impact of violence on human flesh. In a sense, his is an argument about realism. Gone are the impactless deaths of the high fantasy Schwarzenegger and Willis variety, replaced by deaths that carry the freight of genuine trauma, if only fleetingly. Yet the film's overtures towards realism are highly circumspect. Tom's actions in this scene are, despite Cronenberg's suggestion, positively superheroic. The quick emergence of Joey in the seventeen-second gunfight reinserts a strong dose of unreality into the film, just as the opening sequence involving Leland and Billy had previously established the film's tenuous relation to the precepts of cinematic realism. This distance from realism, a distance that is created by establishing and then countering generic expectations, is a hallmark of the film, whch will only accelerate as the scenes of violence become increasingly intense.

Cronenberg's commentary on the DVD raises, briefly, one final issue about the shooting that the film slyly glosses over. He maintains that the killing of Leland and Billy is 'set up to be completely justified.' Certainly, this is true cinematically. Cronenberg deftly moves his audience through a short burst of brutal violence in which viewers are given no time for the kind of sober reflection that the 'consequence shot' is presumed to carry. Like Tom/Joey, the audience is carried along by adrenaline and instinct and also by alertness to the reality of how things play out in movie gunfights: the bad guys get what is coming to them, what they deserve. In the end, Leland and Billy get what all serial killers get: a brutal death at the hands of a righteous man. Their deaths might be justified by the conventions of American cinema, but are they justified otherwise? Are they defensible morally?

There is much that points towards Tom's innocence in this scene. He attempts to find a non-violent outcome, even offering the men money to go on their way. Leland and Billy have uttered clear and unmistakable threats, and Leland has pointed a gun directly at Tom. Billy is shot only after he himself has first fired in the direction of Tom and Mick, the cook. This killing is clearly a case of self-defence. But Leland's killing is not so clear-cut. After shooting Billy, Tom pauses and, for a moment, even seems to relax. At this point Leland stabs Tom in the foot. But as Tom wheels on him, enraged by the pain shooting up his leg, it is clear that Leland has been rendered defenceless. He is prostrate on the ground, weaponless, and unable even to regain a standing position. Tom stands over him with a gun to his head, holding him dead to rights. Then, and only then, Tom shoots him. Leland's death is a premeditated gangland style execution, the first full flowering of Joey in the film. Significantly, as he does in the graphic novel, Tom could simply apprehend Leland at this moment. He could call the sheriff and have him arrested. But he makes the decision not to do so. In that instant, he allows Joey Cusack to surface, acting in a manner that suggests that there is a part of Tom, at least a subconscious part, that would like Joey to be released to the world, would like to be found out. In that moment, Tom invites the mobsters back into his life. Cronenberg quickly cuts from this scene to Tom in the hospital, watching Mick's testimonial to his heroism on television. The audience, like Tom, is carried along, reassured that Tom has done the right thing when, in fact, the moral case seems far from clear-cut. Presumably no jury would convict Tom Stall, but has he actually done the right thing? It is a question that the film does not want the audience to ponder, brushing it quickly aside and allowing it to exist largely unacknowledged as the backdrop to the film's second act, when the source of Tom's heroics is revealed to be his violent, psychopathic past.

Tom's actions and decisions in the diner conclude the first act of the film, and Cronenberg quickly launches us into an entirely new kind of movie, one that has overtones strongly derived from the cinema of Alfred Hitchcock and the fatalism of film noir. Of course, Hitchcock, more than almost any filmmaker working in Hollywood cinema, made movies that were deeply interested in personal identity and misperception. In a number of films, ranging from *Shadow of a Doubt* (1943) to *North by Northwest* (1959), his work explored the possibility that the people that we think we know well might, in fact, be strangers to us, bearing dark, hidden histories and capabilities. The chapter that is opened by the arrival of Carl Fogarty in Tom Stall's diner is just such a case. When Fogarty accuses Tom of being Joey Cusack, two possibilities instantly arise for the viewer: Fogarty is correct, and Tom's fame has led him to be found out; or Fogarty is wrong, and Tom stands accused of being someone that he is not. Unlike Hitchcock's classic formulation of the latter scenario, *The Wrong Man* (1956), Cronenberg leaves the possibilities deliberately open for some time. While Hitchcock opens *The Wrong Man* by personally assuring us that his protagonist has been falsely accused (as if anyone would otherwise believe that Henry Fonda could be a liquor store robber), the ambiguity that is central to *A History of Violence* draws the film more concretely towards the anxiety-producing arena of film noir. And, of course, as events will prove, Carl Fogarty is in no way mistaken about who Tom really is.

Fogarty's certainty seems to be a hallmark of the film noir. The coming and going of violent men through Stall's diner eerily recall the opening of Robert Siodmak's *The Killers* (1946), in which a pair of professional hitmen announce their intention to kill The Swede (Burt Lancaster). Yet *A History of Violence* is not a film noir. Or at least it is not merely a film noir. In the same way that it is not a comic book film, not a serial killer film, not a bully film, not a small family drama, it is about the intersection of all of these generic conventions at once. Many of the classic elements of the film noir are absent from *A History of Violence* – the urban setting (except briefly, in Philadelphia), the low-key lighting, the extreme camera angles and expressionist framing, the deep-focus cinematography, the important use of flashbacks to unpack the narrative. Yet in terms of the more global aspects of noir in terms of themes, mood, and narrative pattern, it is clear that the film owes as much to the noir tradition as to any genre, save, perhaps, the western. Like so many films noir, *A History of Violence* relies on a highly subjective point of view and features a protagonist with starkly shifting roles and an ill-fated relationship to society. And, like so many other films noir, Cronenberg's movie attains something of a thorough indictment not of a single man, but of the entire society that has produced him. If we take seriously the noir influence on *A History of Violence*, we should anticipate discovering a protagonist tainted by a dishonest past that will ultimately condemn him to his doom, a man caught in a hopeless situation, battling forces that threaten to undermine him and that ultimately are revealed to be the product of his own inability to resist temptation. In his decision to execute Leland, Cronenberg first shows us a man unable to resist his own propensity for violence. With the introduction of Fogarty, he ushers in the dishonest past that will spell disaster for this apparently peaceable Indiana family man.

While *A History of Violence* might owe only a conceptual debt to a film like *The Wrong Man*, it is clearly strongly indebted to the noir tradition in general and to a film like *Out of the Past* (1947) in particular. Significantly, in the question-and-answer section of the movie's promotional website (www.historyofviolence.com), Cronenberg is asked directly about his film's relationship to Jacques Tourneur's noir masterpiece: 'Do you feel there's a connection between this movie and the Robert Mitchum movie, *Out of the Past*? I've never seen *Out of the Past*, unfortunately – I've heard that it's a classic film noir – so I can't really say. Just putting the two titles side by side suggests that there's a connection, though.' Like the suggestion that he was unaware that the film was based on a comic book, this response is tough to accept at face value. The mere fact that *Out of the Past* is mentioned on the film's website is a clue to Cronenberg's concerns and ambitions for his own film, especially insofar as that film is about a small-town gas station owner swept up in a murder mystery when his past catches up with him. Nonetheless, *A History of Violence* is hardly an analogue of *Out of the Past*. Just as the film and comic book versions of the story start at a common narrative point and then radically diverge, so too do the films made by Cronenberg and Tourneur. Significantly, the past of Robert Mitchum's Jeff Bailey catches up with him simply by chance when he is spotted by an old associate. Bailey does nothing to bring his Jeff Markham identity back from the past; it simply stumbles across him, as it was fated to do. In *A History of Violence*, however, the fates are slightly more complicated. While it is true that Joey Cusack's identity is revealed only because Leland and Billy just happen to stumble into his diner, bringing him to the attention of the national media, Cronenberg establishes a deeper connection between Joey and the killers that is revealed through subtle gestures such as tidying doorways and the meaningful look exchanged between Leland and Tom. In both films the hero is fated to be discovered, but while Jeff is found out through no fault of his own, Tom is at least partially complicit in bringing Joey into the light through the execution of Leland. The fatalism is present in each film, but it differs slightly in each. In *Out of the Past* Jeff is discovered because America is a small world, while in Cronenberg's film Tom is found out because violence attracts violence.

In the hospital, after the shooting, Tom has become a hero in his community. News of the events is playing on three television channels, and Edie arrives to show him that he has made the front page of the Millbrook Times. As Tom leaves the hospital in a wheelchair, we get the first sense that Millbrook itself is an actual town. Outside of the scenes of Jack at the high school, it would be very easy to come to the conclusion that Millbrook is a town without people, consisting of little more than the Stall house, a main street, and Tom's diner. The group that gathers to applaud Tom provides the first sense that the Stalls are legitimately part of a larger community in Millbrook, and the national media provide the sense that Millbrook itself is still connected to the American nation, if only electronically ('You could probably do Larry King Live, Dad. That would be cool!'). Twice Tom is a called an 'American hero' by the reporter who waits for him as he returns home, reassuring us that Tom's experiences are very much connected to the larger national fabric. Yet, in the scenes immediately following the shooting at the diner, Cronenberg foregrounds Tom's unease in his new role. While Joey has become expert at masquerading as a small-town family man, adding the complication of local hero to that role is much more difficult. It is a part that he wants to quickly move past, as he tells the reporter, and he assures his son that he is no hero, merely a man who got very lucky.

Luck, of course, is not on his side the next day. Once again the community has come out in force in the suddenly crowded Stall diner, where seemingly the whole town has gravitated to bask in the reflected glory of the national hero. Tom is hoping to downplay his new position, but the scene that follows places the idea of masquerade front and centre for the first time when the primary issue of the film – Tom's true identity – is brought to light. As Carl Fogarty and his men enter the diner, Edie initially misidentifies them as reporters. 'They don't look like reporters,' Tom replies. And he, more than anyone, should know. If they don't look like reporters to Tom, it is no surprise, perhaps, that he doesn't look like a hero to them. While ordering black coffee, the same

3.3. Fogarty menaces Tom with the truth. ©MMV, New Line Productions, Inc. All rights reserved. Photo by Takashi Seida. Photo appears courtesy of New Line Productions, Inc.

drink preferred by Leland and Billy and, presumably, all cold-blooded killers, Fogarty taunts Tom with his new guise: 'You're the big hero. You sure took care of those two bad men.' Tom denies this assertion, as he will repeatedly deny his true identity in the scene. Confronted with his past, he does not immediately own up to it, in contrast to *Out of the Past*, but attempts to obfuscate and deny. Six times in this scene Fogarty calls Tom 'Joey,' and each time he is denied. He has never heard of Joey Cusack, he's never been to Philadelphia, he's never met Carl Fogarty or looked upon his damaged face. The menace implied by the presence of these men, whom Edie and Tom separately attempt to hustle out the door, clearly evokes the calm-faced terror posed by a figure like Max Cady (Robert Mitchum) in *Cape Fear* (1962). As in *Out of the Past*, this is a film in which a threat from the past resurfaces to disrupt the small-town life of a good man and his family. However, in the former the protagonist has always been an upstanding citizen, whereas in the latter he is trying to escape a violent, criminal past. It is in the space between these two movies that the 'wrong man' film also comes sharply into relief, as Cronenberg interweaves these three genres to constantly trouble the audience's sense of the actual truth. The threat that Fogarty poses to Tom Stall and his family is immediately identifiable to those in the know. Just as, in *Cape Fear*, Sam Bowden (Gregory Peck) tells police chief Mark Dutton (Martin Balsam) 'You have to know him to feel the threat,' in the Cronenberg film Fogarty is a man whom Joey knows 'intimately,' and so he feels the threat all the more keenly.

As in *Cape Fear* also, the lawyer in the Stall family is on a first-name basis with local law enforcement and requests a favour. When straw-hatted Sheriff Sam Carney (Peter MacNeill) pulls over Fogarty and his men, the masquerading continues. Although they claim to be simple 'tourists' passing through Millbrook, Sam quickly gets to the bottom of who they are. Sitting in the Stall living room later that evening, he identifies the men as Charles Roarke, Frank Mulligan, and Carl Fogarty, mobsters out of Philadelphia. More important than their names, however, is what they truly are: 'They're the real thing. They're bad men,' says Sam. It is in this scene that Sam becomes the second person to raise the possibility that Tom might not be who he says he is, when he enquires about the possibility that Tom might be in some sort of witness protection program. Sam is right to suspect that Tom, who is not originally from the tight-knit Millbrook community, might have a secret to hide, but he is unable, at least at this moment, to imagine that Tom might also be 'the real thing.' Millbrook, after all, is, as he tells Fogarty, a 'nice town. We have nice people here. We take care of our nice people.' Insofar as he believes this to be true, Sam regards Tom as one of the nice people that he takes care of, a fact that he reaffirms to the Stalls when he assures them, 'we look out for our own here.' With the town's support firmly established, the connections between A History of Violence and Cape Fear grow stronger. Both films feature a small-town family fighting with the support of local law enforcement against a former convict who has emerged from the past to threaten the sanctity of the family unit. More specifically, Cronenberg's film echoes Cape Fear very specifically insofar as Fogarty, like Cady in the earlier film, is too smart to make explicit threats or to step afoul of the law. But it is not yet clear if Stall is an innocent victim, like Sam Bowden, or a man whose past has caught up to him, like Jeff Bailey in Out of the Past. What is clear from the knowing play of the tropes of the small-town-stalker genre film is that we have moved beyond the wrong man film and are treading into far more dangerous territory.

What is particularly interesting about this film is that, in the process of shifting generic gears, Cronenberg is remarkably unwilling to truly abandon any of the genre expectations that he has already established. Indeed, genres do not so much displace one another in A History of Violence as they accrue, like layers of paint, one over the other, a constant flurry of new disguises. As a thriller, A History of Violence is remarkably free of many of the hallmarks of that genre and tends to downplay moments of intense excitement that audiences have come to expect in such films. The lone exception to this tendency is the unusual chase sequence that occurs just before the midpoint of the movie. The sequence opens with Tom, limping from the injury he sustained to his foot in the battle with Leland, walking to work at the diner. The framing of the Stall's mailbox and the road in front of the house recalls a similar shot from the opening, suggesting that the film is starting again and that once again Tom's life is about to be troubled by violence. A severely low-angled shot of the diner serves as the transition to Tom alone in the dark, contemplating the situation that he now finds himself in. Significantly, Tom sits at the diner counter in the same seat previously occupied by Leland and by Fogarty. Like those men, Tom drinks coffee. This staging can be somewhat ambiguous to an audience predisposed to the belief that Tom may be the wrong man, but in retrospect it is absolutely evident that Cronenberg is equating Tom with the killers that he has confronted on that stool. Slowly, almost as if shot in slow motion, Tom lifts his head and turns to face the street, but there is a steely glint in his eyes that was previously absent. Cronenberg plays the scene close to his vest, not wanting to tip the audience to Tom's true identity quite yet. It is impossible to say with certainty what he is thinking at this moment, but it seems certain that violence is part of the equation.

As he turns to the street, Tom sees Fogarty's car parked in front of the diner, then slowly pulling away from the curb. Following it outside, he breaks into a run as the mobsters pull further ahead, reaching for his cellphone to place a panic warning call to Edie. At this moment, the audience feels Tom's terror. Trapped on a deserted street, racing on a wounded foot against killers in a car, his helplessness is palpable. Cronenberg quickly establishes a classic, D.W. Griffith-style rescue sequence, using parallel montage to intercut between hero, villain, and the potential victim. Specifically, he offers a series of cuts between Tom and Edie as she is roused from bed by her husband's urgent call. A shot of the Chrysler disappearing over a hill returns us to the menace offered by Fogarty. The sharp tones of the violin music accelerate a sense of panic as Edie struggles to find and load her husband's shotgun in the bedroom closet and as Tom, sweating heavily now, lumbers towards his home and family. Edie races down the stairs, locks the door to the house, and waits, shotgun poised for the threat that never materializes. It is only when Tom stumbles through the door that we, like Tom and Edie, realize that we have been had. Cronenberg has staged a race against no one. When Fogarty and his men disappeared over the hill they did not drive to the Stall house, they simply vanished.

This brief sequence, the non-chase sequence, is one of the clearest enunciations of the film's formal strategy. Cronenberg plays expertly on the audience's expectations here. Because we are fully aware that thrillers have exciting chase sequences, he teases us with our own anticipation, carefully bouncing between the three sets of subjects. The dynamics of the editing rhythm, the shifts from tightly enclosed spaces to Tom as a distant and isolated figure on the roadway, play upon a collective understanding of generic convention. In short, Cronenberg uses a century of 'women in danger' tropes in order to suggest a threat that is not actualized in the narrative. This strategy further helps to solidify audience identification with the Stalls, for just as they are taunted and fooled by Fogarty, so too do we have our expectations thwarted by the filmmaker. Like Tom, we have misread the scene. If our hearts, like his, pound briefly, it is because Hollywood has taught us what to expect in these circumstances, and Cronenberg craftily plays our awareness against us.

A similar set of expectations drives the scene at the mall in which Fogarty confronts Edie. On the DVD commentary, Cronenberg suggests that *A History of Violence* is 'a modern Western,' and further that 'I suppose the mall now stands in for the saloon, or perhaps the general store, that you would find in a Western movie.' This comparison seems inapt, however. While it may be a plausible analogue for the general store, the mall is certainly not a stand-in for the saloon, a space in which we would not expect to find a woman alone with her young daughter. Insofar as the suggestion rings hollow, it highlights, first, the way that this film does not map genre elements onto its structure in direct relationships, and, second, that Cronenberg selects a scene with one of the least direct connections to the western to hint at the existence of these generic conventions in the film. Instead, we are still in the territory occupied by Max Cady, the relentless stalker on the hunt for the Bowden family. In *Cape Fear*, after he kills the Bowden's family dog and assaults a local girl, Cady pursues the young Nancy Bowden (Lori Martin). When he was sent to prison, Max lost his own wife and child, and now he threatens to take his revenge on Sam Bowden through the lawyer's family. Throughout *Cape Fear* there is no doubt that the real danger is not to Sam, but to his daughter Nancy. In this scene, Cronenberg creates a very similar threat to Sarah Stall, made all the more horrifying by the girl's youth. When Fogarty tells Edie 'Nothing to worry about Mrs. Stall, I've been watching over her,' the implied menace carries with it a host of terrible overtones, which the director has made viscerally real to the audience in the opening motel scene. 'You have an enchanting daughter,' says Fogarty: a threat, not a compliment.

Yet the mall scene plays a more important role than merely reinforcing our sense that Fogarty is a legitimate danger. Crucially, it is the scene in which both Edie and the audience begin to suspect that Fogarty might just be telling the truth. Fogarty's speech to Edie establishes, for the first time, the only major facts about his relationship to Joey that the film ever delivers, including the fact that Joey tried to rip out Fogarty's eye with a piece of barbed wire. More important, his speech cuts right to the heart of the film's obsession with identity and masquerade.

Fogarty, it is suggested, is the man who sees through Tom's mask and into his soul, a power seemingly shared by Leland, possibly a trait common among evil and violent men. 'See?' Fogarty asks Edie. 'This isn't a completely dead eye. It still works a bit. The problem is that the only thing I can see with it is Joey Cusack, and it can see right through him. Right through your husband, Edie. See what's inside him, what makes him tick. He's still the same guy. He's still crazy fucking Joey. And you know it, don't you?' Of course, Edie doesn't know it: 'I know that my husband is Tom Stall. That's what I know.' This emphasis on knowing, who we know, and what we know about them, takes on an almost overriding importance here. For Edie, and for the audience, the possibility still exists that Fogarty is simply mistaken, that this scenario remains Hitchcockian, although Edie's strong denials, mixed now with the slightest tinges of doubt, arrive at the same time as the wrong man scenario is winding down. Tom's fiction is collapsing around him, and so, at the same time, the film itself is beginning to abandon the conventions of the wrong man film. Exhausted, this genre must be traded for another. Perhaps this is why Cronenberg, in his commentary, goes out of his way to compare this scene, a classic trope of the wrong man film, to a western. The generic conventions are set here, but they are about to shift dramatically.

Central to Cronenberg's selective mobilization of generic conventions is his choice to frequently abandon the story elements that he has introduced. In some cases, as he did with Leland and Billy, he simply brings the storyline to a close and opens up a new one. But the bully storyline involving Jack is not so much wrapped up as it is transmuted into something completely different. The last time that we see Bobby and his sidekick is midway through the film, immediately following the confrontation between Edie and Fogarty. As Jack and his friend Judy exit a classroom, Bobby shoves Jack from behind, looking to instigate the fight that, by this point, has been twice thwarted. Bobby's taunts cut right to

3.4. Edie and Sarah flee from Fogarty at the mall. ©MMV, New Line Productions, Inc. All rights reserved. Photo by Takashi Seida. Photo appears courtesy of New Line Productions, Inc.

the heart of Jack's insecurities: 'I guess your old man's some kind of tough guy, huh? What's he think of his wimp son? You think he'd take this shit? You think he'd make jokes?.' When Bobby notes that Jack is 'getting mad,' Cronenberg provides a foreshadowing of Joey Cusack's angry visage on the face of his son. Jack squares his shoulders, sets his mouth, and his eyes, cast ever so slightly downward, glower at the bully. At the same time, however, he remains peaceable and is talked into walking away by an obviously intimidated Judy. When Bobby's sidekick once again stops him, however, the situation changes, and he launches a surprise attack on the duo, seizing the advantage with a kick to the groin, before pummelling Bobby into brutal submission in the high school hallway.

Jack's transformation in this scene marks him as a newly powerful persona. No longer the puny scapegoat pushed around by the all-American jock bully, Jack emerges as a proud son determined now to live up to the new image that he has of his father: strong, controlling, dominant, and unafraid. Yet this is not the image that his father has chosen to project. Indeed, it is one that he would do almost anything to repress. When we cut to Jack and Tom discussing the events at the school, the father is outraged by his son's behaviour, while the son is newly confident, abrasive, and not intimidated by his father. 'I only got suspended,' Jack explains, the light punishment regarded as a kind of moral and legal sanction of his acts. Besides, Bobby is 'a jerk,' and in the cinematic logic of the high school bully film, jerks get beaten up when the worm turns, just as everyday heroes in action thrillers blow away the bad men. In responding to his father's concerns, Jack acts out a minor variation of the righteousness that he attributes to the patriarch. Yet this new attitude is fragile and shatters quickly. 'Listen smart mouth,' Tom tells his son, 'in this family we do not solve our problems by hitting people.' 'No,' Jack replies, 'in this family we shoot them.' It is an impudent line that evokes a quick laugh from the audience, but when Tom instinctively slaps his son for it, the audience is shocked back into silence. Cronenberg has hinted throughout the film that Fogarty might be on to the truth about Joey, and with this slap we begin to feel confident that this is not the Hitchcockian wrong man. Jack may have vanquished the bully, but with the strike of his father's hand, he too has just learned that there are more ominous forms of violence in the world. His father is the real bully now.

The second act concludes with the confrontation between Tom and Fogarty on the steps of the Stall house. Cronenberg's commentary has already highlighted the strong undercurrent of the western in this film, albeit at a point where it is not recognizable. Rather, it is through this scene, in which the homestead is defended from bad men, that the film adds yet another layer of Hollywood generic violence. That they are mobsters who have come calling rather than cowboys of the open range hoping to drive off the sodbusters only marginally complicates a showdown that cinema has rendered quintessentially American.

As in the diner scene, there are no shades of moral grey here. Fogarty and his men have Jack and are threatening to kill him. They are, as we have been told, 'bad men,' and Tom's defence of his home and family is portrayed not merely as justifiable, but as commendable. Rising to meet his tormentors, Tom seemingly recalls every great western gunfighter who tried to put away his six-shooters but brandished them one final time when the cause was just. George Stevens's Shane (1953) is one such film, in which the eponymous hero (Alan Ladd) rides to the rescue of the homesteading Starrett family. Like Tom, Shane is a man with a largely undisclosed history of violence, an expert at killing men who is desperately trying to put it all behind him. But unlike Shane, Tom is a man who believes that violence and family might possibly be reconcilable. Shane tells Marian Starrett (Jean Arthur) that 'a gun is as good or as bad as the man using it,' but his departure at the end of the film tells us he no longer believes that to be true. He is fully aware that a gun cor-

3.5. Fogarty and his men arrive for the gunfight. ©MMV, New Line
Productions, Inc. All rights reserved. Photo by Takashi Seida. Photo
appears courtesy of New Line Productions, Inc.

rupts those who live by it, and that taking the life of another changes a man forever. Tom Stall may know this as well, but at this point he still desperately hopes that it is not the case. Both *Shane* and *A History of Violence* are films about violent men forced by circumstances to return to that life if only to protect the peaceful existence of the family. Shane realizes that doing so means that he can never be a part of that family, and he rides off into the sunset, oblivious to little Joey Starrett's cries for his return. By contrast, Joey Cusack still dreams of finding salvation in the arms of his family.

Thus, it is significant that Tom is transformed into Joey while holding his wife, and then reverts to his Tom persona after his son kills Fogarty. It is also significant that Jack's shotgun blast saves not only his father, but a man he now knows to be a cold-blooded killer. It is Joey who, in what he feels will be his last words, confirms his true identity to both Fogarty and his family with 'I should have killed you back in Philly.' Jack, standing just behind, reacts in horror to the truth as much as to his own actions. Moreover, as his father rises from the ground, pistol in hand and face spattered with blood, he has become the totalizing visage of violence that Jack only barely glimpsed earlier that afternoon. It is the murderous Joey who wrenches the shotgun out of Jack's hands, and Jack is right to feel threatened by the presence of this outsider in the Stall home. In one of the film's few self-conscious shots, Cronenberg cuts quickly to a view of the carnage from a dirty second-floor window, where flies buzz at the panes trying to fathom a way outside. With this he frames Jack's flight reflex perfectly, highlighting the torment felt by the teenager whose life has been so dramatically transformed. Joey, for his part, seems torn between a number of options. For a moment he looks as if he might even be contemplating killing Jack to bury the truth about his identity once again. At another moment he perhaps considers congratulating his son, welcoming him into a fraternity of killers. But in the end it is clear that Joey, like Tom, loves his son deeply, and so he tries to comfort him, holding onto Jack and allowing the outward signs of Joey to dissipate in the hope that his family will not be lost to him forever. While the first act ended with his family seeing him as a hero, the second concludes with their knowledge of the much darker truth.

The film's third act, like the second, opens in Tom's hospital room, but little else remains the same. This time Edie does not bound in to see her wounded husband, but slinks into the room, partially hiding from him behind the door. She does not ask how he is recovering, opting instead to ask the questions that Carl Fogarty placed in her head and that the gunfight confirmed for her. 'Tell me the truth,' she demands. Joey hopes that the mask might still be in place: 'Truth?,' he asks. This is the last of his lies to his wife. He wonders what she heard, but, as it is for the audience, the reality is all about what she saw. The physical transformation of Tom into Joey has brought the truth to light: her husband is not a man who killed to defend his friends and his way of life, but a man who killed for money, who killed because he enjoyed it. Yet for Tom, there is still a distinction to be made. He does not want to be Joey anymore. He would prefer to wear the mask of Tom around Millbrook. And Tom is clear that it is, in fact, a mask. When Edie asks him if he is some sort of 'multiple personality schizoid? It's like flipping a switch back and forth for you?' he responds with an explanation that draws upon the language of evangelical Christians: 'I thought I killed Joey Cusack. I went out to the desert and killed him. I spent three years becoming Tom Stall. You have to know this: I wasn't really born again until I met you. I was nothing.' In his mind, Tom has replaced Joey. Of course, as the previous scene has amply demonstrated, nothing could be further from the truth.

Tom's identity is central to this scene, and, indeed, this scene is one of the most important in the film, despite its brevity. In the classic film noir formulation, when the past finally catches up with the hero, we are treated to an elaborate flashback. Jeff Bailey tells Ann Miller (Virginia Huston) such a tale in *Out of the Past*, and Tom McKenna tells his wife his true story in the graphic novel version of *A History of Violence*. But Cronenberg's film is not really a film noir; it only feels like one at times. The lack of a flashback, of course, leaves something of a hole in the overall structure of the tale, but it is clear that hole remains deliberately open. Instead of a fully fleshed out understanding of who Joey was, and how he became Tom, we glean mere fragments of the story that mesh with the little we know from Fogarty's testimony about 'crazy, fucking Joey.' We know that Joey killed for money, and he killed for enjoyment. He took the name 'Tom Stall' because 'it was available.' The image that comes to light from this hospital room is of an incredibly violent man, a man that even Carl Fogarty has reason to fear. With this knowledge, the viewer is empowered with the ability to fill in almost any version of Joey's past that can be imagined. Joey's youth is a blank canvas upon which the viewer can paint the details, substituting any of the too wild and hotheaded gangster characters that have filled the cinematic imagination from Tom Powers and Little Caesar to Sonny Corleone and Tony Montana.

Edie's departure at the end of the scene tells us everything we need to know about the state of the Stall marriage. When Tom returns home, by cab, several days later, both his world and his identity are in tatters. Confronted by Jack on his front step, Tom has lost the patriarchal authority that he had only recently gained with his 'heroic' murder of Leland and Billy. Jack has returned to being sarcastic with him, reacting bitterly to his new knowledge of his father's identity as 'some sort of closet mobster-dad.' This is our first glimpse of Jack since he killed Fogarty, and it is clear that the act has transformed him. While Jack's victory over Bobby made him cockily elated, his new status as killer has made him withdrawn, morose, and hostile towards his father. As he taunts Tom with the suggestion that he himself will become a gangster and deliver 'a cut' to his father, it is clear that Jack has come full circle: he is the bully now. 'Please son, don't,' Tom begs as his son taunts him, but Jack can treat his father now only as he himself has learned to treat others in high school, with teasing and threats: 'If I talk to Sam about you, will you have me whacked?' These are the last words spoken between Jack and Tom in the film, a coldly acerbic deconstruction of the father-son bond.

Entering his home, Tom suddenly realizes that he doesn't belong there and that he has nowhere left to go. When the sheriff arrives, Tom agrees to speak to him about the facts in the case that 'just don't fit.' Sam, like Jack and Edie, has figured out the truth about Joey. Recognizing that Fogarty had not made a mistake, Sam tries to draw the real story out of Tom, until Edie intercedes on her husband's behalf. Just as he is about to speak up, to confess his crimes to Sam and put aside the shambles that has been his middle-American masquerade, Edie slips back into the role of devoted housewife: 'Sam you've got too much time on your hands. Tom is ... Tom is who he says he is, and that's all that matters. Sam, hasn't this family suffered enough?' With this, Edie begins to cry on her husband's shoulder, creating an uneasy scene in the family living room that obliges Sam to take his leave, even though all three participants in the conversation are clearly aware that she is performing the role of the distraught housewife only as a stalling tactic. Edie plays at the 'helpless woman' role from a position of strength, self-consciously mimicking the way that she now knows her husband has played at the role of peaceable family man from a position of violence. With this performance, the wrong man scenario, like the bully story before it, has played itself out in its entirety, and even the noir trappings fade away in the scene of rough sex on the stairs. Richie's phone call will transport the film once again into new territory, bringing it fully into the traditions of the gangster revenge film with western shoot-out overtones.

3.6. Tom and Jack: A fractured relationship. ©MMV, New Line Productions, Inc. All rights reserved. Photo by Takashi Seida. Photo appears courtesy of New Line Productions, Inc.

At the end of Hitchcock's *The Wrong Man*, when the real culprit is apprehended, Manny Balestrero (Henry Fonda) asks for no vengeance, but seeks merely to shame the guilty man, asking him 'Do you know what you've done to my wife?' At the conclusion of *Cape Fear*, Sam Bowden doesn't take the life of Max Cady, choosing instead to have him live 'a long life in a cage.' And in *The Killers*, when the gunmen come for Swede Anderson, he simply allows them to end his life and his misery. While *A History of Violence* owes a great deal to these cinematic precedents, its conclusion is cut from different cloth entirely, drawing on a number of classic revenge films from both the noir and the western traditions. In Fritz Lang's *Fury* (1936), for instance, Joe Wilson (Spencer Tracy) is accused of a crime that he did not commit and is subsequently lynched by an angry mob, but when he survives the fire that should have killed him, he takes revenge by allowing members of the mob to stand trial for his murder. Similarly, in *Hang 'Em High* (1968), Jed Cooper (Clint Eastwood) is accused of cattle rustling and is unsuccessfully hanged for the crime. He later returns to his former profession as a lawman and brings the culprits to justice. These films, which feature wrong men falsely accused, focus alternately on the ethics of vengeance and on justice as a form of reparation for the wrong that has been done to the hero. Key to each, however, is the fact that the hero is legitimately an innocent man who has done nothing wrong, but who, nonetheless, has been asked to pay a very high price.

A different, and much more violent, scenario is found in John Boorman's neo-noir *Point Blank* (1967), in which Walker (Lee Marvin) works his way up the executive ladder of a sinister corporation after he is cheated out of $93,000 in a heist, shot, and left for dead. Significantly, Walker is not an innocent man, but one who has participated in a criminal act, during which time he was double-crossed by his wife and his partner. It is Walker's criminality that seemingly authorizes his cold-blooded retribution, as he is a character who was already damned before he was betrayed. Of course, this is also true of Joey Cusack. He is not the wrong man, an innocent asked by Fogarty to pay an unjust price for another man's crime. Fogarty's grievance is legitimate: as we will learn from Richie, Joey broke up his club, killed his men, and tried to rip out his eye with a piece of barbed wire. He is not, like Manny Balestrero, a victim of misidentification by witnesses and police corruption; nor is he, like Sam Bowden, a good man who was only doing his job. There-fore, he is in no situation to occupy the moral high ground and allow justice to take its course. Rather, while Tom may play the wrong man, he is, in point of fact, more akin to Walker, a dangerously wronged criminal who now must work his way up the chain of command in order to put his life back together the way that he wants it.

The road back to Philadelphia is a long one for Joey Cusack. He departs in the middle of the night and arrives after driving non-stop 'pretty much fifteen, sixteen hours.' But more than that, it is a trip that takes him back twenty years, to the place in which he was raised and where his true identity was forged. In the bar, when Ruben asks if he is Joey, he can now answer truthfully for the first time in the film: 'Yeah, I'm Joey. So what do we do now?' If Tom had fashioned himself as some sort of retired gunfighter, the Joey who sits with Ruben in the Track and Turf is a gangster through and through. In most respects, Joey's trip east is an inversion of the western archetype that so structures the film. Throughout, however, violence has moved towards the east like the weather. Leland and Billy were heading east when they arrived in Mil-ford, and now Joey has been drawn further east, by a call from his past. From this standpoint, it seems as if the tropes of the west are returning to the city to confront it, the perfect collision of the western and the big-city gangster drama. By the time Joey enters Ruben's escalade, the film has completely adopted a new generic skin.

As Cronenberg points out in the DVD commentary, one of the inter-esting things about the third act is that it is almost entirely uncued by the first two-thirds of the film. Sam mentions Richie Cusack to Tom and Edie when he first fills them in on the details about Fogarty and his men, but the reference is fleeting and passes easily. Similarly, Fogarty suggests to Edie that she ask Tom about 'his older brother, Richie,' but the thread is not pursued until much later in the film. Thus, as Joey rides along with Ruben, the viewer has little sense of what to expect. Indeed, unless the viewer specifically recalls William Hurt's name from the opening credits and is still awaiting his arrival, the scene plays as a total enigma, a blank slate upon which any sort of violence might be written. The conventions of the thriller assure us that the final act will be the most violent, but we are given little clue about what sort of history will unfold here. As Joey asks, what do we do now?

From the standpoint of the convention of the Hollywood thriller, the introduction of mob boss Richie Cusack, 'a very upscale kind of guy,' in the words of Ruben, should fill the audience with dread. Here, after all, is the ultimate villain – a man to whom even the vicious Carl Fogarty answers. Yet, at the same time, we know next to nothing about Richie. From the standpoint of generic expectation, we anticipate that each villain will pose a more vexing problem for the hero than the one preceding, a formula that bodes ill for Joey Cusack, who has been wounded successively more gravely in each of his fights in the film up to this point. Nonetheless, in specific narrative terms, Cronenberg has significantly downplayed the threat of each of his villains, increasingly relying on genre convention to allow the audience to fill in the details. Thus, we witness the evil that is Billy and Leland in the office of the motel, but we are informed only obliquely, by Sam, of Fogarty's past crimes. For Richie, however, we lack even that information. Because of where he appears in the narrative, we are conditioned to expect to find a monster, but we have no clues to what kind.

Joey and Richie, of course, are a study in opposites, diametrically opposed on almost every level: austere/ostentatious, reserved/gregarious, married/gay. While the film does not explicitly detail Richie's homosexuality, and while he endlessly discusses women as potential sexual conquests, the film works overtime to code the baddest of the bad men as a gay man by placing him in an opulently subdued home, with well-dressed and well-coifed henchmen at his beck and call. Hurt plays the role to the campy hilt, portraying Richie as a man-sniffing dandy whose hopelessness with a gun is a stark contrast to Joey's feral hyper-masculine capabilities. Cronenberg does not shy away from the question of Richie's sexuality on his director's commentary: 'I was wanting to suggest that there was more going on in this household than just a gangster with his henchman, that there was some strange thing going on. I wouldn't have said that it was necessarily gay gangster perverse, but it pleased Viggo to think that when he was trying to figure out how to play the relationship.' Interestingly, a case, however tenuous, could be made for the suggestion that virtually every significant villain in *A History of Violence* is queer. Leland and Billy spend their nights together in out-of-the-way motels. Fogarty, like Richie, surrounds himself with the company of men. Even Bobby, who suggests that it is Jack who is a 'faggot,' is constantly accompanied not by a girlfriend, but by his accommodating sidekick. This is not to suggest that each of these characters is, in fact, gay, but I do wish to draw attention to the particular manner in which the film presents violence and villainy with homosexual and homosocial overtones.

Gay villains are hardly a rarity in Cronenberg films, and the director has made a career of killing off his queer characters, as Christine Ramsay has so well documented.[4] No analysis of Cronenberg seems complete without detailing the homophobia that runs through his films. In *The Romance of Transgression in Canada*, Tom Waugh succinctly summed up the filmmaker's contribution to Canadian queer cinema, stating that he cannot 'exclude the obsessive homophobe who can't stay away, the publicly funded Canadian exporter of images of corporeal and sexual

3.7. William Hurt as Richie Cusack. ©MMV, New Line Productions, Inc. All rights reserved. Photo by Takashi Seida. Photo appears courtesy of New Line Productions, Inc.

perversity around the world, whether as strip miner and sanitizer of queer canons ... or as mythologizer of queer revulsion ... and existential despair ... Cronenberg resolves the stress by littering the landscape with dead queers.'[5] A History of Violence is no different. In the end, the monster that we find is marked not so much by violence, but by his sexuality.

A History of Violence is a narrative that strives to identify the heart of violence in American society or at least in American film culture, and it ultimately locates the source of evil in the corruption of the patriarchal, heterosexual, middle-class family. In the mob film genre, the dual sense of family becomes pertinent in explaining the hostility towards Joey that emanates from Richie, his blood, and Fogarty, a member of the gangster family. The question that is placed on the table by the set design, casting, and costuming of the scenes at Cusack Manor is whether Richie's sexuality, which Cronenberg works so hard to foreground, is merely evidence of the corruption in the Cusack family or else its cause. One of the difficulties in answering such a question is the fact that the film obfuscates so much of the family. Even at the end we learn little about what it is that Joey had done to incur Fogarty's wrath and force him into hiding for so long. What little additional information we glean from Richie is contained in a single stretch of dialogue: 'You bust up a made man's place. You kill some of his guys. You take his eye. Jesus, Joey, you took his eye.' Of course, almost none of this is new information. Instead, the film plays with our sense of mob family as it has been developed from the Corleones to the Sopranos in order to highlight a sense of family as a matrix of resentments and obligations.

Even more than needing Richie as a gay man, Cronenberg acknowledges that he needed the two as brothers. This is a change from the graphic novel and from Olson's original script that Cronenberg brought to the picture as a shorthand way to suggest a deep and complex history between the two. Just as the film relentlessly evokes various cinematic genres as a means of directing the action of the film and the reaction of the viewer without having to spell out every minor detail, so too does the familial relationship allow Cronenberg to hint at depths that are not explicitly sounded by the film itself. In the confrontation in Richie's office, the latter is outwardly curious about what has become of his brother after all these years, quietly hopeful that Joey might return to the fold and openly resentful that he has cost him 'a lot of time and money.' Despite his plush surroundings, Richie feels that he could have achieved more, and more easily, if only his brother had not acted inappropriately. In the end, it is resentment that dominates Richie's relationship with his brother, much as it has since the day Joey was born: 'You always were a problem for me, Joey. When Mom brought you home from the hospital I tried to strangle you in your crib.' For Richie, like so many cinematic gangsters, the bonds of brotherhood pale in comparison with the drive towards personal glory and a consciousness of 'family' in a depersonalized and mythic sense. In his reaction to Joey's avowals of personal happiness in his new Indiana lifestyle, Richie recalls the famous dictum of Michael Corleone (Al Pacino) speaking to Fredo (John Cazale) in *The Godfather* (1972) 'you're my older brother, and I love you. But don't ever take sides with anyone against the family again. Ever.' The difference is that in Joey's case he is the younger brother, and it is not so clear that Richie loves him.

The vaulted ceilings and dark brown trappings lend Richie's house a strong resemblance to that of another Irish mafia boss, Leo O'Bannon (Albert Finney) in the Coen brothers' *Miller's Crossing* (1990), a mob film that also included a series of gay gangsters. This likeness seems apt, given the way that the penultimate scene of *A History of Violence* slides into the sort of darkly oddball slapstick humour and tweaking of generic expectations that has become a hallmark of the Coens. The battle between Joey and Richie is largely a tale of two different films. On the one hand, Joey performs like a superhero throughout. When he is garroted from behind, he is able to block the killer's strike and with kicks to disable two armed gunmen. He dispatches them while dodging bullets from Richie's gun and snaps the neck of a third henchman before shooting a fourth. In each of his three violent encounters, which have included a steadily growing number of opponents – beginning with two in the diner, three at his home, and five, including Richie, in this scene – Joey fights spectacularly, but now his performance crosses into the absurd theatrics generally reserved for the *Die Hard* movies. Joey is a ruthless killing machine: smarter, faster, stronger, and more lethal than any man could be.

Richie, on the other hand, is revealed to be completely useless in the ways of violence. Although Cronenberg has set us up to anticipate a fierce battle from Richie as the ruthless beast at the end of the trail of monsters, he is, in fact, merely pathetic. He watches in disgust as his henchmen are roughed up, but he himself misses Joey with a series of five bullets fired from near pointblank range. Subsequently, he is fooled by an open door and eliminated from the fight when he is locked out of his own mansion. He is ultimately killed by his brother while holding his gun in the crook of his arm, where he has placed it as he is stumbling for his keys and a way back into his house. It is a comic spectacle and one that serves to diminish Richie as a threat in our eyes. Yet, if Richie is not the bad man at the end of the trail, who is? All evidence points to the fact that it is Joey, not Richie, who is the true source of evil in the film, the boy who should have been strangled in his crib.

As the sun rises, Joey heads to the small lake on the property, strips to the waist, and throws away the gun with which he has executed his brother. For the third time in the film, and for the first time unmistakably, the cross that hangs from his neck is visible, a quiet reminder of the role of faith in Joey's life as a born-again Tom. As he washes the day's events away, the question of whether he can be re-baptized one final time remains. This is the question that the film only hints at. Cronenberg cuts quickly to Joey returning to the Stall family home, where Edie and the children sit mutely inside, eating dinner. Joey's return freezes Edie and Jack, each reacting with a show of apprehension and fear of this man. As he enters the kitchen, Edie declines to meet Joey's gaze, holding her head low and refusing to acknowledge him. Jack behaves the same, never once looking in his father's direction. And so it falls to little Sarah Stall to decide whether this killer will be admitted back into the family or cast out forever. She rises, gathers her father's plate and cutlery, and sets the table for him. As Joey sits with his family, Jack reaches out to offer him the meatloaf, and Edie, finally, and with tears in her eyes, raises her face to look into the eyes of this stranger in their midst, looking across the table and finding the teary face of the man that they will pretend is Tom Stall.

The final scene of *A History of Violence* is played entirely without dialogue, and consequently it is carried entirely by the blocking and performances of the actors. Nothing is said to assure us of the final resolution of Tom Stall's history. In his commentary on the DVD, Cronenberg relates the fact that the last page of the shooting script contained only two words: 'There's hope.' Nonetheless, whatever hope remains in the film seems far-fetched, given the ordeal that the film has just put these characters, and the audience, through. Indeed, one of the strongest conventions of the film noir, and the source of its ability to engage in social criticism of any sort, is the ambiguous ending. The noir narrative is one that confronts the hero with an awareness that things are not what they seem and that people are not who they claim to be. As Lee Horsley has written, 'In the course of the story, it becomes clear that the things that are amiss cannot be dealt with rationally and cannot ultimately be put to rights. The dispersal of guilt, the instability of roles, and the difficulties of grasping the events taking place all mean that there can be no "simple solution." Even if there is a gesture in the direction of a happy ending, the group reformed is damaged and cannot return to prior innocence.'[6] This description perfectly describes the conclusion of Cronenberg's film, all the more so because of the way that *A History of Violence* plays at processes of generic masking. Just as Joey once again adopts the mask of Tom Stall, even for a family that can now see through the fiction, so too does Cronenberg adopt the mask of a hopeful ending, even for an audience grown accustomed to his manipulations of convention.

To buy into the hopeful ending that Cronenberg describes is to believe that Joey Cusack can disavow his violent self in a way that he could not when challenged to do so first by Leland and Billy, then by Fogarty, and finally by Richie. 'Joey,' Shane tells the young Scarrett boy who has grown to idolize him, 'there's no living with it, with the killing. There's no going back from it. Right or wrong, it's a brand. A brand that sticks. There's no going back.' The American western film is rife with gunmen who recognize that their day has passed, who ride off into the sunset in the full awareness that they would sacrifice themselves so that the people whom they love might find ways to live that do not include gun fighting. From John Ford's *The Man Who Shot Liberty Valance* (1962) to Clint Eastwood's *Unforgiven* (1992), the western has proven a rich genre for the investigation of the myth of the American male and the centrality of violence and gun culture in the forging of American notions of family and nation. Few film genres speak as plainly and directly to American mythologies as the western, which is, perhaps, why Cronenberg repeatedly evokes the genre in his commentary, despite the lack of obvious western trappings in the film. For instance, in discussing Howard Shore's score for the film, he says that the music 'has some hints of great American music from American western movies – John Ford, Howard Hawks.' The citation of Hawks and Ford as stylistic influences is particularly telling about the film's intention to be read as a western, not as much in genre trappings as in tone. Indeed, as Robert B. Ray has highlighted, the western, more than many genres, is particularly flexible and available to trans-genre experimentation.[7] The lack of formal narrative expectations and the reliance on visual idioms in the construction of the western highlight the way that it is easily evoked as a sensibility, an ideology, or a disposition towards notions of American individualism, family, and nation. The mere presence of a horse beside the Stall barn seems enough to confirm Cronenberg's sense that *A History of Violence* is, at least in part, a highly revisionist western or, to use Ray's term, a 'disguised western.'

The gunfighter logic that animates so many westerns plays a part in a particularly fascinating moral sleight of hand. Inevitably, the western endorses a neo-Darwinian logic associated with the survival of the fastest. Hollywood's desire for happy endings or, at the very least, ambiguous endings in which the hero survives to fight another day necessitates a structure in which the hero is inevitably the fastest gun in the west, shooting down the villain in a climactic showdown. This has the tendency of equating technical proficiency with a weapon with moral superiority, justice, and righteousness, even at the cost of some internal narrative coherence. Thus, in *Shane*, to take but one example, the survival-of-the-fastest law holds when Shane guns down the amoral killer-for-hire, Jack Wilson (Jack Palance), at the film's conclusion, but not when Wilson kills Frank Torey (Elisha Cook, Jr), a scene in which the moral high ground is occupied by the out-gunned homesteader. 'That was,' as Richard Corliss observes about *A History of Violence*, 'just the way that, in national and movie mythology, the West was won.'[8] Darwinism, of course, is a famously amoral world view wherein survival goes not to the righteous, but to the fittest and strongest. It is this amorality that the western seeks to disavow by placing power in the hands of the just.

Darwinism and the myth of the American west have gone hand in hand at least since Frederick Jackson Turner delivered his essay 'The Significance of the Frontier in American History' at the 1893 Chicago World's Fair. Turner's 'frontier thesis' drew on an evolutionary model to explain that the frontier, the region between civilized society (urbanity)

3.8. Tom as the western gunfighter protecting the homestead. ©MMV,
New Line Productions, Inc. All rights reserved. Photo by Takashi Seida.
Photo appears courtesy of New Line Productions, Inc.

and the untamed wilderness, was the source of American exceptionalism. Turner argued that, with every generation that moved westward from the coast, European traditions were lost and new distinctly American ones were formed. Thus, each generation that moved west became more 'American,' specifically more democratic, less tolerant of hierarchy, more individualistic, more distrustful of authority, and, significantly, more violent. This popular and enduring equation of the frontier with America and American values as a whole has had the effect of reinforcing certain ideological associations that are common to the western. Consequently, to make a western film, or even a partial pseudo-western, as Cronenberg has done here, is to make a film that has something to say about the American dream and national values.

Late in the film, Richie highlights the degree to which *A History of Violence* is a story about America when he observes about Joey, 'You're living the American dream. You really bought into it, didn't you?' Indeed, Joey really has, and Cronenberg uses the clash between his past and his aspirations for the future as a means, as Manohla Dargis notes in *New York Times*, to explore 'the myth and meaning of America (or at least a representative facsimile) through its dreams, nightmares and compulsive frenzies.'[9] Yet what, precisely, do these explorations lead to? In unsettling the traditions of the western, perhaps the most triumphalist of Hollywood genres, by combining it with the tropes of other genres of cinematic violence, what does the film have to say about the myth and meaning of America?

Centrally, *A History of Violence* is concerned with the shifting nature of heroism in contemporary America. Very early on in the film, Cronenberg leads us to believe that this will be the film's central theme. When Tom kills Leland and Billy, he is hailed as a national hero on a series of television stations and in newspaper headlines, and he is greeted as a champion by a crowd gathered outside the local hospital. Moreover, Tom's heroism apparently rubs off on his star-struck son, as he suddenly discovers a new side to himself by standing up to Bobby. In mobilizing the wrong man scenario, Cronenberg allows us to imagine for a brief moment a film that is very much about the intersection of fame and heroism and the consequences for a community of glorifying violence. Yet this is clearly not what the film is about at all.

As Joey walks back into the Stall household at the end of the movie, the question of whether he was ever a hero is posed in important ways. Without his ruthless past as a hitman, he never would have had the speed and skill to dispatch the criminals in the diner. In short, it is his violent past that saves both him and his family. Yet for Joey to remain a hero to his family and, by extension, to the viewer, it is necessary that his acts of violence be condoned or sanctioned in some manner. Generally, in both movies and real life, that sanction takes the form of God, country and family, and this film is no exception. Tom kills Leland and Billy because they threaten his friends and his business. He later kills Fogarty, because if he does not, he knows that Fogarty will kill his family. But can the same be said of Richie and his men? Joey seems justified in his actions, since, after all, they are in the process of trying to kill him. And certainly Richie's initial question on the phone, 'You going to come to see me, or do I have to come see you?' implies a threat to the Stall family. Or does it?

Like the execution of the unarmed Leland, the killing of Richie and his men exists on a different moral plain than the killings during the shoot-out do. Significantly, the killing of Fogarty, perhaps the only morally straightforward murder in the film, is actually accomplished by Jack, not Joey. In this way the film suggests that violence is not the best solution, but is actually part of the problem. As we learn in retrospect, it is Joey, not Tom, who kills Billy, and it is Joey whose ruthless instincts kick in when Leland is killed. Once the initial trigger is pulled and Joey is released into Millbrook, the entire moral equation is abandoned. Tom might like to think that he has acted to protect his family, but it is made clear from his actions in Philadelphia that Joey is protecting Joey. He fights the mob in Pennsylvania so that he doesn't have to fight the mob in Indiana. His pre-emptive strike is not presented as such – 'I'm here to make peace,' he unconvincingly says to his brother – but it seems clear that he has moved well past heroism into the realm of vigilantism.

The shift from hero to vigilante happens in a heartbeat, so subtly that the audience is left no time to reflect upon it, but it is crucial to the meaning of the film. Cronenberg relies upon cinematic tropes to establish scenes in which it seems only natural that the villains should be dispatched by the fastest gun in the room, but on closer inspection the morality of these decisions appears deeply flawed. Joey's rationale for killing the other men so he can remain Tom Stall does not make his actions heroic or even justifiable any more than it did when he killed for profit and for pleasure in his earlier life. While the film seemingly draws upon an initial presumption that some people are naturally evil and deserve to be shot, it upsets this notion by allowing Joey Cusack, the fittest, fastest, and most violent of the film's characters, to survive and beg for forgiveness merely because he has a family and now wears a Christian cross around his neck. In a film that relentlessly demonstrates how violence begets further violence, Cronenberg is also at pains to illustrate how easily we can be led to embrace violence and immorality to protect what we cherish. In the end, Tom is not a hero in this film, nor is his cause just, and Cronenberg leaves us with the question: just who are we rooting for in this film?

This is, of course, the same question that Edie poses when she confronts her husband after the shoot-out with Fogarty. The identity issue is of paramount importance in *A History of Violence*, and it raises the related question of whether or not a family can live with the cold, hard truth that their titular head is a killer. The hospital room conversation between Edie and Joey revolves around a tension that derives from her sense of a stable identity and Joey's concept of the possibility that a man can remake himself. For Joey, adopting the identity of Tom was a painful undertaking that he equates with death and rebirth: a slow, deliberate process of reconstruction that is, in fact, one of the promises of America. For Edie, on the other hand, the sudden loss of identity is jarring: 'Our name, Jesus Christ, my name. Jack's name. Sarah's name. Stall. Tom Stall. Did you just make that up? Where did that name come from?' In Edie's case, the truth does not immediately set her free; rather, it fundamentally undermines her own sense of self and her rootedness within the community. The revelation that her very name is arbitrary compromises her own sense of identity.

Joey's identity, on the other hand, seems remarkably stable in retrospect. As the film unfolds, it invites the audience to consider at least the possibility that Tom Stall is losing himself amid the confusion that surrounds his relationship to Joey Cusack. Yet by the end of the film, when we have been exposed to the full reality of who Joey is, it is easy to see that Tom Stall never existed except as a role that Joey successfully played for decades. Just as his family begrudgingly lets him back into the home, knowing what they know, the audience also realizes that they have always known they were watching Joey even when they hoped it was really Tom. If Tom were who he said he was, he would have perished in his diner at the hands of Leland and Billy. Instead, it is Joey Cusack, professional killer, who is the 'American hero.' Moreover, it is Joey who is the authentic self. When Richie asks, 'Hey, when you dream, are you still Joey?' it seems to be a question intended to befuddle the audience, since they have not been given access to the character's interior mind. Yet in retrospect, the answer is simple: of course he is still Joey. The violence at the diner does not draw Joey out of Tom, but simply begins the process of unmasking Joey to the world.

To that end, perhaps the most pressing question asked by the film concerns forgiveness. In a perceptive review of the film in *The Nation*, Stuart Klawans reminds us that 'women and children everywhere live

3.9. The real face of Joey Cusack. ©MMV, New Line Productions, Inc. All rights reserved. Photo by Takashi Seida. Photo appears courtesy of New Line Productions, Inc.

with men who are killers,'[10] or, more specifically, they live with men who were soldiers, men who 'did what they had to do.' Living with killers, Klawans suggests, is not a difficulty. What is troubling is when that killing is not sanctioned by a sense of a larger purpose. Absent that larger purpose, Joey Cusack is a man with little hope of redemption. He is, after all, a guilty man living with a family of innocents. Further, his guilt has been visited upon the people he loves, and they have been scarred by the consequences of his choices, becoming liars, cheaters, and even killers themselves in order to help to save him from himself. He is not, as the film so relentlessly teases in the first half, the wrong man, but they are the wrong family. They are singled out to pay for crimes that they had nothing to do with, and that they could not possibly have known about. In this way they recall the mute little girl killed in the opening scene, helpless victims of forces beyond their comprehension. It is no coincidence that the film concludes with a scene featuring another mute little girl that mirrors the opening. We are forced to wonder: has Joey ended Sarah's childhood, just as Billy ended that of the other girl?

The cross that he wears throughout the film initially leads us to see Tom as an innocent man, but by the end it more pertinently suggests that Joey will be crucified for his sins. While the initials 'J.C.' in any work of fiction always invite speculation about Jesus metaphors, A History of Violence is, as Ken Tucker notes, an 'interestingly irreligious heartland movie.'[11] There is no question that Joey makes a horribly inappropriate substitute for the Christian saviour. Yet the central question posed by the ending of the film is tremendously resonant with the Christian sensibility at the heart of so much American mythologizing: can Joey's family forgive him, and, perhaps more appropriately, should they? Writing in the liberal Catholic magazine Commonweal, Richard Alleva identifies the film's central theme as 'Is a person allowed forgiveness for an immoral past after he demonstrates a genuinely reformed character and a willingness to live in society peacefully and even benevolently, but does not make legal reparations for specific crimes?' It is a fascinating question, but mistaken in one of its central premises: what evidence is given to suggest that Joey Cusack is genuinely reformed? Alleva regards as a central shortcoming of the film the fact that the protagonist remains too ambiguous: 'For his plight to truly move us, we would have to be privy to how he experienced a profound conversion years before the events in the film.'[12] For this to happen, we would need the noir-style flashback that Cronenberg so conspicuously denies us, a denial that highlights a difference between the intentions of the filmmaker and the desires of the film critic. A History of Violence, it seems, is a film not about the moral redemption of Tom Stall, but about the moral downfall of his family. More specifically, it asks us to consider the cost that must be paid to maintain the family as the moral centre of America. Writing in Rolling Stone, film critic Peter Travers describes the themes of the film as innately American: 'Cronenberg knows Americans have a history of violence. It's wired into our DNA. Without a hint of sermonizing, he shows how we secretly crave what we publicly condemn, and how we even make peace with it. The family tableau that ends the film is as chilling and redemptive as anything Cronenberg has ever crafted.'[13] Sitting at their dinner table, the Stall family opts to ignore the violence that needs to occur elsewhere for them to be allowed to continue to live their lives in peace. In the end, A History of Violence is a film not about forgiving, but about forgetting.

Travers's contention that violence is America's secret craving accords nicely with the possibility that A History of Violence is not quite the realist examination of family dynamics that it initially seems to be. Indeed, the unreality of the film, its occasional lapses into implausible action sequences and other unlikely scenarios, highlights the possibility that an entirely different sort of interpretation is required to get to the bottom it. Writing in Sight and Sound, Graham Fuller offers one of the least conventional, but most interesting, readings of the film when he suggests that the action that unfolds is largely the dream life of Tom Stall, a film in which 'the dark side of the American psyche emerges into the light.' Fuller suggests that the narrative of A History of Violence amounts to little more than a dream, or the daydreams of Tom and of his son Jack, each emasculated in reality but longing for a life in which they are virile men. Tom, though he is a lowly diner owner with an ambitious and successful wife, imagines that he could be the type of man who stands up to his rich, dismissive brother, who ravishes his wife, and who is hailed as a national hero for his action-man-style gunplay. In short, he dreams that he could be Shane. Similarly, Jack imagines that he could make the decisive play in a baseball game, beat the daylights out of the bully who torments him, and save the life of his father. One of the biggest problems with Fuller's thesis, however, is the way that these competing dreams intersect. How, for example, can we reconcile Tom's fantasy serial killers meeting with Jack's bully on the streets of Millford? Fuller is not able to fully resolve these problems, offering only that 'the demarcations between these reveries are vague, and it isn't always clear who is experiencing them' as a way of explaining away the apparent inconsistency that mars his thesis.[14] Yet even if his argument fails to truly persuade the reader that A History of Violence is a large-scale fantasy akin to The Secret Life of Walter Mitty (1947) or Billy Liar (1963), films in which impotent men fantasize about virility, he usefully highlights the sheer unreality of the proceedings and the important ways that Cronenberg indulges his taste for the fantastic even within a largely realist framework.

Fuller's contention that Jack's 'unexpected lurch into swift, decisive violence is unlikely for such a gentle, highly strung boy - except, of course, in a movie' seems paramount to understanding the film.[15] Central to the logic of A History of Violence is a sense of postmodern self-awareness, the assuredness that the type of violence that the film addresses is movie violence, rather than that of the real world. In this way, the unreality of the America portrayed in the film, the self-consciously Norman-Rockwell-styled Middle America, can be productively compared to other films depicting a darkness behind the façade of normality. Cronenberg's work here is commonly compared to that of David Lynch, who, in films like *Blue Velvet* (1986) and *Mulholland Drive* (2001) highlighted the constructedness of American normalcy. From this point of view, Cronenberg has not made the most realist film of his career, but has made a movie that itself is a commentary on notions of cinematic realism. The arch self-awareness of Lynch might seem at odds with Cronenbergian cinema, which most often expresses itself as a particularly idiosyncratic form of wide-angled expressionism, yet in a film about masked identities the logic seems to make perfect sense.

In short, if *A History of Violence* seems to lack a certain generic stability, this might be explained by the collision of its postmodern sensibility and art film aspirations. Despite its large budget, it is clear that the film aspires to exist in the same rarified cinematic air as the non-commercial and critically lauded films that Cronenberg has since focused upon, at least *Dead Ringers* and *Naked Lunch*. He has not, as many critics and arts writers maintain, returned to the Hollywood model in order to produce a typical blockbuster thriller, but has tied the conventions of the thriller to those of the western, the film noir, the gangster film, the high school bully movie, and the serial killer film in a way that comments upon each one without ever fully embracing the conventions of any. Cronenberg moves through each as a way of unsettling viewer expectations about narrative, but without ever fully departing from a cause-and-effect structure. To this end, the film might seem to be little more than a postmodern excavation of the history of cinematic violence. In its focus on narrative causality, *A History of Violence* is at odds with the classic definition of the 'art film.' *Chicago Reader* critic Jonathan Rosenbaum stresses the tension between art and genre when he asks: 'Is *A History of Violence* a popular genre movie, soliciting visceral, unthinking responses to its violence while evoking westerns and noirs? Or is it an art film, reflecting on the meaning, implications, and effects of its violence, and getting us to do the same?'[16] Rosenbaum concludes that, despite the filmmaker's 'genius,' the conventions of these two cinematic modes are irreconcilable. Following that line of reasoning, it might be fair to say that the movie seemingly evokes the traits of the art film, particularly the investigation of personal identity, without actually embracing them. In this way, Cronenberg treats the art film as a genre like all the others. It is not privileged as the meta-genre that holds the whole project together; rather, it is simply another element in the long catalogue of cinematic tropes mobilized by the film.

The question remains: is there a single unifying framework through which this film can be made comprehensible? Certainly, auteurism holds out some hope as one such possibility. The deft combination of techniques characterizing the narrative style of the art film and the classic Hollywood movie seems at once both a hallmark of postmodern cinematic practice generally and the career of David Cronenberg specifically. Despite having incorporated a wide range of filmmaking styles and practices, from the high modernist *Stereo* to the low pulp of *The Brood*, and seemingly every stop in between, Cronenberg, more than almost any other Canadian filmmaker, is widely considered to evince, as William Beard argues, 'a high degree of consistency in its thematic concerns, distinct trademarks in its subject matter, considerable evidence of artistic self-consciousness, and a notably expressive cinematic technique.'[17] Similarly, Peter Morris highlights the way that Cronenberg is a filmmaker who has 'remained dogmatically loyal to his artistic vision, which, among other things, insisted that there was no difference between high art and popular culture.'[18] These and other critics have long emphasized how Cronenberg's career can, and perhaps should, be read in unified terms, despite its many dramatic shifts in tone, genre, theme, and subject matter. Nonetheless, *A History of Violence*, which the director has openly characterized as a work-for-hire project, holds the possibility of problematizing this integrated view of the filmmaker's career by introducing atypical elements and approaches. In short, the question becomes whether this film is a departure from the filmmaker's customary concerns, an extension of those traditions, or something else entirely.

More than many filmmakers, Cronenberg is highly self-conscious about his role as an 'auteur,' and in his interviews he stresses the importance of his own sensibility within his work. Speaking of another work-for-hire film set in the United States, *The Dead Zone*, Cronenberg describes his influence on the text as a subtle shading of detail: 'I didn't try to impose myself on the subject-matter. I had to assume that through the accumulation of the thousands and thousands of details that go into making a film, I would be there. And obviously I chose to do the project.'[19] William Beard has pinpointed the specific recurrent themes and ideas that tend to define the Cronenberg project as centrally related to the unconscious mind and a mind/body duality. For Beard, repression is one of the keys to understanding Cronenberg's work. Thus, he contends that the brood in the movie of the same name represents Nola's 'repressed anger'; that 'repression and avoidance are at the centre' of *The Dead Zone*; that in *Dead Ringers* the ego-self 'stands threatened by a frightening, self-dissolving power that lurks perpetually (perhaps dormant, but always there) in the shadows of its own psychic environment'; and that the path taken by Gallimard in *M. Butterfly* 'from repression to liberation to catastrophe replicates one more time the trajectory of the Cronenberg hero.'[20] In short, Beard argues that the tension between repression and liberation is – alongside the duality of good and evil, mind and body, id and superego – the central opposition that structures the filmmaker's work. Certainly, *A History of Violence* can be easily reconciled to this vision. Central to the dynamic of this film is

Tom Stall's repression of Joey Cusack, of his own personal history of violence, and of his aggressive impulses. Those tendencies are unleashed
by the arrival of Leland and Billy in his diner, and the ensuing events
transform him into the man that he once was, with disastrous consequences for his family. Beard terms Cronenberg's first feature, *Stereo*, a
'catastrophe of over-liberation,' and the same phrase might be applied
to *A History of Violence*, a film in which Joey is unable to escape who he is
when the repressed returns with a vengeance.

One key to reconciling *A History of Violence* within the Cronenbergian
fascination with repression is an awareness of the filmmaker's sense of
biology as destiny. On the one hand, if the troubles that arrive on Tom
Stall's doorstep seem predestined, that may be simply a function of the
generic requirements of the fatalism of film noir; on the other hand,
the theme of destiny coincides with the director's well-developed
thoughts on the construction of identities. While critics have argued
that in the 'nature versus nurture' debate, particularly insofar as issues
of sexual difference are at stake, 'Cronenberg continues to hold firmly
to the nature side.'[21] The filmmaker himself has repeatedly talked
about his idea that humans have the power to transform themselves in
a manner that seems to belie this easy sense of biological determinism:
'I'm talking about the possibility that human beings would be able to
physically mutate at will, even if it took five years to complete that
mutation. Sheer force of will would allow you to change your physical
self'[22]. This concept of the human body resonates strongly across *A History of Violence*, a film in which Viggo Mortensen's performance holds
the key to the true identity of Tom/Joey. Indeed, this film seems to
demonstrate Cronenberg's thesis, but only to a limited extent. In the
end, when push comes to shove, Joey's transformation is revealed as
incomplete, and he is unable to hold onto the Tom Stall identity that he
has struggled for twenty years to cultivate. Further, the way that the
film works to connect Joey's violence to Jack's and, even further, Joey's

to Richie's seems to suggest a biological predisposition to violence that is handed down from generation to generation.

The possibility that violence is an inherited trait infuses the politics of the film with a certain bleak pessimism and more closely ties the movie to a classic concept of Cronenberg as a filmmaker. Although published five years before A History of Violence was filmed, Barbara Creed's words seem descriptive of Tom Stall: 'While Cronenberg's characters similarly live in bizarre – sometimes paranoid – fantasy worlds, their desire to experience states of symbiotic union, bliss or transcendence is not part of a larger plan to save the world. Rather, the journey of these solitary figures is an intensely personal one – although the transformation they seek similarly involves a degree of bodily alteration and feminization'[23]. Nothing could be clearer than the fact that Tom has no desire to save the world. While he is depicted as a good neighbour and respected local citizen, Tom shuns the hero label and focuses his attention almost exclusively on his family, without any commensurate social obligation. Indeed, Tom feels so little obligation to the world at large that he has allowed his mobster enemies to flourish for more than two decades, so long as they left him and his family in peace. Tom is the classic Cronenbergian hero described by Creed, a solitary man whose decision to forsake violence has enabled his feminization, a process that the events of the film will radically undo. Thus, the construction of Tom Stall as an isolated and repressed hero who will undergo a transformative identity shift seems to highlight the important ways that A History of Violence can be read as an extension of canonical Cronenbergian themes. At the same time, however, certain formal tendencies in the film seem to suggest that this movie does not fit into the auteurist box so neatly.

Discussing Rabid in The Artist as Monster, Beard asks:

Why are powerful males pushed to the margins as shadowy, elusive patriarchal scientists, and the centre of the narratives occupied weakly by these 'nice,' well-intentioned, ineffective characters? I believe it is because the authorial sensibility sees power – narrative and artistic – as invested in the objects of desire, namely sexual females, while being unable as yet to accept responsibility as the originator of the texts' desire and, simultaneously, rejecting the heroic male mythology of Hollywood narrative.[24]

Beard argues that Cronenberg is interested in displacing the heroic and action-oriented male lead in his films because his own tendencies are at odds with the dominant narrative traditions of Hollywood. While this might be the case with Cronenberg's work of the 1970s, it is not clear that such a theory applies to a film like A History of Violence, whose take-charge male lead attempts to solve all of his problems through hyper-aggressive masculine violence. Further, if Cronenberg is sceptical of classical narrative norms, as Beard suggests, this film troubles that reticence. A History of Violence has at least the appearance of a classical narrative, or several classical narratives, despite the fact that each feint towards generic stability proves troubling when seen in light of later events in the film. If Cronenberg's is a cinema of weak-willed male heroes and non-traditional narrative structures, which is certainly the case in films like eXistenZ and Naked Lunch, can we regard A History of Violence as a truly Cronenbergian film?

One solution to this conundrum resides in the dual figure of Tom/Joey. In movies like The Fly, Cronenberg located the central conflict within the interior psychological life of the male lead. Specifically, the ineffective male lead, Seth Brundle (Jeff Goldblum), through a science experiment run amok, is invested with tremendous physical powers that eventually undo him. A History of Violence follows a somewhat similar pattern, but with important distinctions. As in The Fly, the primary conflict in the film plays out in the transformation of the psychology of the male hero, as he changes from a passive figure into a man of action.

Yet, while Brundle is a victim of his fate, the same cannot so easily be said about Tom. Indeed, Tom is not a quiet figure at all, but a vicious killer simply masquerading as passive. The transformation of Brundle adds something new to the scientist: powers and a newfound confidence that were previously absent. But the transformation of Tom to Joey adds nothing new to his character, it simply reveals to the world what was already present. Thematically, this is a significant shift, demonstrating that *A History of Violence* does not neatly sit within a tradition of emasculated male heroes in Cronenberg's films.

One reason for this difference relates to the question of heroism. It is fair to ask whether, in fact, Tom/Joey is actually the hero of this film. John Harkness has argued that, with the exception of *Videodrome*, 'the villains in Cronenberg's films are not his scientists, but outsiders to the central world of the characters.'[25] Certainly, on one level this is true of *A History of Violence*, which works hard to create a sense that the various killers who come to Millbrook are aliens in that society. In this way, the film easily falls into the horror tradition that is reliant on external threats. At the same time, however, an argument can be made that Joey is not the hero of the film, but is simply another one of the villains. Cronenberg opens this interpretation by relentlessly twinning Joey with the other killers, highlighting a secret, coded brotherhood among them. From this perspective, the film can be read as a horror movie in which the evil is located internally, within the family and, indeed, within Tom himself, a man who is in no way what he outwardly appears to be. Following the logic that regards Joey not as a hero, but as the villain to whom the other characters reconcile, *A History of Violence* departs from the norms of the Cronenberg canon while at the same time maintaining an outward façade of fidelity to his themes. On the question of the location of evil, this film only pretends to be Cronenbergian. Not only is the hero merely pretending to be emasculated, but he is also only pretending to be heroic.

Of course, the most striking difference between this film and the 'typical' Cronenberg movie has to do with the absence of those moments that have come to be defined as quintessentially Cronenbergian. The moments of visceral bodily trauma that have punctuated his work since his days as the director of low-budget schlock horror films are the hallmarks that have come to define the filmmaker's particular sensibility, yet they are almost completely absent from A History of Violence. The most visually disturbing images in the film are the brief glimpses that we are provided of the aftermath of violent acts committed by the Stall men: Leland's destroyed face in the diner, Bobby's bloody mouth in the high school hallway, the horribly mangled nose of Fogarty's gunman, and so on. Still, in comparison with the corporeal horrors inflicted upon audiences by Cronenberg in earlier works such as The Fly and Existenz, these are seeming trifles, merely brief glimpses of a deeper, more disturbing form of horror that is anticipated by the film without ever being fully delivered. In this way, Cronenberg's refusal to provide the fully 'Cronenbergian Moment' and his constantly teasing suggestion of it accord nicely with the film's various nods to generic expectations that remain similarly unfulfilled. In these brief glimpses of viscera, the filmmaker seems to be letting the audience know that he is fully aware of their expectations, but is also telling them that he will not deliver the goods. In this way, A History of Violence makes overtures to the traditions of the Cronenberg film without fully embracing those traditions. Just as the film is not really a noir, or a western, or a gangster film, so too it masquerades at times as a Cronenberg movie without ever fully committing to that position.

Interestingly, the absence of a signature grotesque Cronenberg moment in A History of Violence is addressed, to a certain degree, on the DVD release of the film. Among the several special features on the disc is 'Scene 44,' the sole deleted scene included. This scene, which takes place immediately after Sam informs the Stalls of Fogarty's identity and then leaves, places the viewer in Tom's head in the form of a dream sequence. The dream goes a long way towards answering Richie's question about his brother's true identity, for when Tom dreams in this scene he is shown very clearly to be Joey. Scene 44 opens with Fogarty once again seated at the diner, his sunglasses in place. It is night, and the diner is devoid of other patrons – Fogarty and Joey are alone. In a plain, emotionless voice Fogarty speaks: 'I'm going to kill you. And everyone you know. Your whole goddamned family.' Joey responds in a similarly affectless manner. He slowly turns and puts down the coffee pot that he holds, replacing it with a shotgun. He then calmly turns his attention towards Fogarty, levels the gun at his chest and fires. Fogarty is thrown from his stool, sailing across the diner floor and coming to rest in a heap. Tom leaps over the counter and, gun in hand, approaches the giggling mobster. Fogarty's chest has been blown apart, his ribs and entrails visible and smoking. Slowly he raises his own pistol, takes aim and fires at Joey, who awakens suddenly from his nightmare.

In several ways, Scene 44 would considerably strengthen the overall structure of the film. Joey's switch from a coffee pot, the weapon with which he dispatched Leland, to a shotgun, the weapon with which Jack will kill Fogarty, is symbolic of the increased threat to his well-being and that of his family as the specifics of his past catch up with him. Further, the scene, with its bluntly stated threat from Fogarty, allows the audience to realize along with Joey that his past will return to destroy his present. Nonetheless, the increased clarity and foreshadowing that the scene provides comes, as Cronenberg notes in his commentary, with a price. Significantly, the dream sequence places the viewer in Joey's mind for the first and only time. Moreover, it does so at a juncture in the film where his identity is still very much up in the air. To this point, Cronenberg has only hinted that Tom is really Joey, but the dream sequence seems to confirm it once and for all. This revelation would rob the transformation on the front lawn of much of its power, thereby

3.10. Tom and Fogarty face off in a dream. ©MMV, New Line Productions, Inc. All rights reserved. Photo by Takashi Seida. Photo appears courtesy of New Line Productions, Inc.

deflating some of the film's larger themes. In the end, the director opted to delete the scene, reasoning, 'it felt like it was from some other movie.'

That other movie, of course, would be a Cronenberg movie. Indeed, the director is very up front about the fact that Scene 44, with its smoking chest wound, is emblematic of his style: 'It's the kind of scene that people might think that I would demand, in fact, to have in a movie ... people think I have a checklist of things I must have, but really I don't.' According to Cronenberg, the nightmare sequence was a part of the script as Josh Olson originally drafted it, and its visceral Cronenbergian overtones were simply coincidental and had nothing to do with his interest in the project. This recalls the director's repeated claims that he had no idea that his film was an adaptation of a comic book, and that, therefore, the particularly gruesome image from that original work, the presumed dead friend resurrected as a limbless torture puppet for the mob, similarly played no role in attracting the director. If we take the filmmaker at his word, neither of these sets of images plays an important role in shaping the work or his relationship to the material. Not only is Scene 44 included, but it was actually completed, even scored, for the DVD. Further, it is also made the subject of the only 'making of' feature on the DVD. The question naturally follows: why would they make a DVD featurette for a scene that is not only not a part of the movie, but according to the director not even a part of his overall vision?

It seems clear from the lavish attention paid to Scene 44 on the DVD that the suppression of the Cronenbergian Moment in this film is a central element of the movie's logic. Just as the occasional icy glance from Tom reveals the presence of Joey, the lavish attention paid to Scene 44 on the DVD seems to tip off something of the director's actual interests and desires. *A History of Violence* is a film that very consciously works to raise and then undermine audience expectations. The rapid dispatch of the initial serial killers, the chase sequence from the diner to the Stall homestead that turns out to have no villain involved – these and other sequences serve to establish generic conventions that are then almost immediately frustrated. At the same time, the film strategically plays with the audience's preconceived expectations of what will happen in a film directed by David Cronenberg. In the scenes of violence, there is a palpable possibility that something Cronenbergian just might happen, but it never does, or it barely does. If we return to William Beard's observation about Cronenberg's aversion to both powerful men and Hollywood conventions, it is worth noting the way that he productively ties narrative power to the creative power of the director, equating the filmmaker with his heroes more forthrightly than many critics might do. Nonetheless, in a case like this, it seems entirely apt to suggest a close connection between filmmaker and lead character, because, as the film continues to undermine auteurist conventions, it becomes clear that Cronenberg may be masquerading in this film in the same way that Tom is. It seems that Scene 44 is deleted from *A History of Violence* not because it reveals Joey too soon, but because it reveals David Cronenberg too obviously.

The 'reality' of David Cronenberg is something that is deliberately shrouded from the audience of *A History of Violence*, a knowing rejection of the kinds of assumptions about him that widely circulate, and a self-conscious adoption of the kind of cinephiliac narrative strategy that he most often avoids. Fanned by the subjects and themes of his films, Cronenberg's public persona is that of a reserved 'nice guy' whose inner life seems darkly perverse. Shortly after the release of *A History of Violence* a news story began to circulate on the Internet entitled 'Cronenberg's Public Sex.' The article claims that the director hoped to place Mortensen and Bello at ease for the film's two sex scenes by performing them with his wife in front of the cast and crew. Complete with quotes from a 'freaked out' Mortensen, the hoax, which was subsequently debunked by the *New York Times*, played upon a widely held public perception of Cronenberg's deviant take on human sexuality. Indeed, sexuality is a crucial component of the director's work. Beard notes running themes of 'omnisexuality,' the malleability of sexual roles that pervade all but a small handful of Cronenberg's films.[26] Further, sexuality is one of the most thoroughly mined avenues of investigation in Cronenberg scholarship. Frequently, that scholarship has highlighted a perception that the director's work reveals what Robin Wood diagnoses as a fear and hatred of human sexuality,[27] and few filmmakers have made sexuality so central to their thematic concerns as has Cronenberg in films such as *Dead Ringers* and *Crash*. In an interview with Chris Rodley, he explains the relationship of sex and death in his work: 'sexuality is one of those very basic issues. Life and death and sexuality are interlinked. You can't discuss one without in some way discussing the others.'[28] It is not surprising, therefore, that the pivotal issues regarding truth and masquerade in *A History of Violence* are played out so clearly not in the instances of killing, but in the film's twinned sex scenes.

In *Weird Sex and Snowshoes*, Katherine Monk suggests that Cronenberg's films 'give the woman the dominant role' during sex scenes,[29] and this is certainly true of *A History of Violence*. The first of these scenes occurs early in the film, preceding any suggestion that Tom Stall is not who he claims to be: a small-town diner owner. Immediately following the scene in which Jack is terrorized by Bobby after gym class, the film shifts from the scary reality of high school to an erotic fantasy of the same. Meeting her husband outside the diner on the darkened main street of Millbrook, Edie takes Tom on a date intended to make up for the fact that 'we never got to be teenagers together.' Back at their home, Edie comes to bed dressed in a cheerleader outfit, and the central theme of masquerade is placed front and centre by the film. 'What have you done with my wife?' Tom asks, maintaining his role as husband and father in spite of Edie's role playing. Still in the performance,

3.11. Edie prepares to seduce her husband. ©MMV, New Line Productions, Inc. All rights reserved. Photo by Takashi Seida. Photo appears courtesy of New Line Productions, Inc.

she cautions him, 'Quiet, my parents are in the next room,' and when he replies, 'you're naughty,' it is clear that he has entered the game that she is playing. The extended sex scene, with its focus on mutuality and a shared fantasy, is highly ironic in retrospect. Edie is playful when she tells Tom 'you are such a bad boy,' but it is only later that the depths of his badness will be fully revealed to her. Similarly, the post-coital scene, in which the couple spoons while talking about the depths of their love for each other, is filled with moments of dark foreshadowing. 'I'm the luckiest son of a bitch alive,' says Tom, basking in the glow of his loving wife. 'You are the best man I've ever known. There's no luck involved,' she replies, a sentiment that will, by the conclusion of the film, be revealed as an unwitting lie.

In the film's second sex scene, Edie no longer believes her husband to be the best man she's ever known, but, on the contrary, suspects that he may, in fact, be the worst. The moment that 'brings the sex-violence nexus to the boiling point,'[31] as Manohla Dargis suggests in a lengthy *New York Times* article about this single scene, occurs after the departure of Sam, when Edie has defended Joey by performing the role of the sobbing wife. Again, Cronenberg introduces sexuality into the film by coupling it with masquerade and role playing, but in this scene that pretence is quickly abandoned. As Edie moves to go upstairs, she is followed by Tom, who attempts to talk to her. When she is pinned against the wall at the foot of the stairs, Edie whirls on her husband, slapping him in the face. He responds by grabbing her by the throat, suddenly and dramatically reverting back to his Joey identity. She recognizes this instantly, sneering at him: 'Fuck you, Joey.' They continue to fight on the stairs, he strangling her, she slapping him again, until, unexpectedly, she pulls him closer to her and kisses him. What follows is a rough sex scene on the stairs, Edie and Joey's sexual encounter quite at odds with tenderness displayed by Tom and Edie earlier in the film. Indeed, many critics read the scene as a rape. Robert S. Miller, for example, situates the scene, in which Edie seemingly consents, to a cinematic history that includes *Gone With the Wind* (1939) and *The Fountainhead* (1943), films in which powerful men ravish the women that they love.[31] For his part, Cronenberg maintained in interviews that the scene was not a rape: "'Will the scene on the stairs be perceived as a rape?' because it's not supposed to be a rape, it's supposed to be a very complex act on both their parts.'[32] The complexity of the scene is highlighted by the divergent readings that it generates. During the course of the scene Mortensen is transformed from Tom to Joey and, once he has finished, back to Tom, a performance that highlights the Cronenbergian association of sex and death to an exceptional degree. The sequence drives home the point that, stripped of all the illusions, Tom is a mere fiction and Joey is the authentic personality. Reduced to primal urges in the face of sex and death, Joey is revealed to be no more Tom than Edie is still a cheerleader. The first sex scene demonstrates how people can agree to wear masks, while the second emphasizes that masks can obscure the truth only for so long.

Yet the stairway scene raises a few questions, just as it provides answers about the identity of Tom/Joey. Notably, it asks the audience to reconsider their understanding of Edie and of her particular desires at this point in the film. Monk argues that 'all sex in Cronenberg movies is transformative, and usually in a bad way,'[35] and this seems particularly true in this scene as it pertains to Edie. As the film plays with the conventions of the film noir, the two most noteworthy generic absences are the revelatory flashback and the femme fatale. A common trope within the genre, the femme fatale is a noteworthy absence from *A History of Violence*, problematizing its noirish aspirations. Yet in the rough sex scene we are shown a very different vision of Edie Stall than has been presented up to that point. Significantly, she manipulates the local police officer with a cunningly calculated performance that she is able to turn on and off like any classic noir heroine. More important, in turning her battle with Joey into a violent sexual encounter, Edie her-self is transformed from loving and supportive wife into what Dargis terms 'a gangster's moll with a taste for a little rough trade.'[34]

In an extremely insightful commentary on this scene, Dargis high-lights the way that Cronenberg places the camera in the most voyeuris-tic position possible, distancing the viewer from the sex, but also forcing the audience to reconsider not only Joey, but Edie as well: 'In a story of blood and vengeance, Mr. Cronenberg asks us to look at those who pick up guns in our name, protectors who whisper they love us with hands around our throats. And then, with this scene, he goes one better and asks us to look at those who open their hearts and bare themselves to such a killing love.'[35] Dargis highlights the moral culpa-bility of Edie that is revealed in this scene, a position suggestive of the classic femme fatale who betrays the noir hero, thereby sealing his fate. If Edie seals the fate of anyone, it is that of Tom, the man who first betrayed her with his lies. In accepting the truth about Joey, Edie dooms the part of him that is Tom to irrelevance. Whatever else hap-pens, now that the truth is known, the fantasy of 'the best man I've ever known' holds weight no longer. And, at the same time, her own moral assuredness is thrown into question. Certainly, the quick shot of Edie rocking herself in her bedroom, her back badly bruised, indicates that she has quickly lost the taste for rough trade identified by Dargis.

The tension between fantasy and reality that lies at the heart of these two scenes obviously is crucial to the structure of the film as a whole. Indeed, one could plausibly suggest that these scenes are the most important in the entire work. As Cronenberg himself describes it in an interview with Serge Grünberg, 'We called that married sex and gangster sex. But the married sex is also a fantasy, where they decide to play roles to excite themselves, roles that they never played with each other. So, the whole question of identity in sexuality and violence in sexuality is there in those two scenes.'[36] It is significant, therefore, that neither scene was included in the earliest drafts of the screenplay. According to an article in *Written By*, the magazine of the Writer's Guild of America, Josh Olson added the scenes in a deliberate effort to give the film more of a Cronenbergian feeling: 'I wanted it to be a Cronenberg film. I didn't see any way to come up with biological mutations in this story. There weren't any sex scenes in the original draft. I knew he's good at dark, violent sex. So I told David I want it to feel like a Cronenberg film, and I was going to write a sex scene that would fit his oeuvre.'[37] Yet in the attempt to tie the script more closely to the style of the director who was now attached to the project, the issue of masquerading once again surfaced. According to Olson, Cronenberg himself had reservations about this new direction in the screenplay: 'He said, "I don't want it to be too "Cronenbergy."'[38] In drafting a pair of scenes intended to cut to the core of his director's personal style, the screenwriter is warned off by that same director. In writing scenes that will reveal the true spirit of his characters, Cronenberg suggests a desire to conceal his own nature in the process by making a film that does not rely too much on his personal trademarks. If Olson was playing at writing in the 'Cronenberg style,' it is also apparent that the filmmaker himself was very consciously trying to play the role of Hollywood director-for-hire and downplay the signature elements that would make this film an auteurist work.

The idea of concealing the truth about oneself is central to arguments about masquerade generally. The masquerade is a concept that was introduced to explain gender differences by Joan Riviere in a 1929 article entitled 'Womanliness as Masquerade.' Arguing from a psychoanalytic position, she suggested that the feminine mask concealed the female's theft of the phallus: 'womanliness therefore could be assumed and worn as a mask.'[39] For Riviere, there was no essential difference between 'genuine womanliness' and the masquerade; the two were mutually bound. In opposition, masculinity was assumed to be fixed and authentic, so that any use of the masquerade in the masculine tradition was assumed to lead to processes of the feminization of the male masquerader. This notion aligns nicely with a figure like Joey Cusack, who, in adopting the mask of Tom Stall, allows himself to be feminized to a large degree, opting for a life of quiet passivity with a wife who is the real breadwinner and head of the family. Nonetheless, Riviere's concept of gender difference has been largely displaced by subsequent scholarship. Distinctions between biological sex and social gender laid the foundation for a rethinking of masculinity and femininity as roles, the performance or enactment of a persona that is separate from the actor. This separation of the individual from behaviour was favoured by sociologists such as Talcott Parsons, who argued that feminine and masculine gender roles were complementary. However, the concept was criticized by feminist scholars who saw a system of domination in Parsons's notion of complementarity and who argued for a concept of multiple gender roles, rather than a solitary and fixed gender role. Judith Butler's notion of gender as performative – that is to say, gender is not something that we are but something that we do – emphasizes the social construction of gender in a more radical form. For Butler, the performance of gender is an artifice that does not mask a natural or true identity. This is at odds with the concept of the masquerade, which suggests, as Harry Brod observes, that 'behind the façade of the mask lies the *real* face, to be revealed when the masquerade is over.'[40] Of course, Brod's concept fits *A History of Violence* more accurately than Butler's does, for when the film draws to a close, it is the real face of Joey Cusack that is the last image we see before the screen fades to black.

It is possible to read *A History of Violence* as a film that is acutely concerned about the masculine masquerade and the transformation of Tom Stall from an inauthentic and therefore feminized man to someone who represents a naturalized form of aggressive masculine violence. In his essay on Alfred Hitchcock's *North by Northwest*, Steven

Cohan details the way that Roger Thornhill (Cary Grant), by masquerading as George Kaplan, is transformed into 'a full-fledged male hero who acts rather than reacts.'[41] Cohan argues that the 1950s was a period in which masculinity was seen to be in crisis, an era in which men had become weak as a result of a dependence on others; consequently, they placed the nation in danger during the Cold War period. In this light, Thornhill's over-attachment to his mother and secretary are cast as a problem of national significance, which is resolved only when Thornhill willingly adopts the Kaplan persona, saves the girl, vanquishes the villain, and thus averts a threat to America's national security. The question arises: given the connections established between Cronenberg's film and the Hitchcockian tradition, should we read *A History of Violence* in light of *North by Northwest*? That is to say, if Roger Thornhill typified the 1950s male as an urban advertising executive in need of toughening up, does Joey Cusack represent the 2000s American male as a man of action who needs to be reawakened? On the other hand, is *A History of Violence* a warning about rousing that sleeping beast?

North by Northwest is largely unambiguous in its politics. All the consequences of Thornhill's turn to action are positive, and he is rewarded for his willingness to take command of the situation in which he finds himself. Tom Stall, however, loses everything because of his decision, whether considered or instinctual, to exert control over the threats to his life and to his family. Most critics see in *A History of Violence* some form of critique of the contemporary United States, particularly of its cultural love affair with violence and its geopolitical instincts towards imperialism. However, it is not always clear precisely what these critics think that the film is saying. The *Washington Post*'s Desson Thomson suggests that the film 'is essentially forcing us to confront troubling questions. Is killing excused by moral imperative? Where does heroism end and vigilantism begin?' But he offers no suggestion as to what answers the film might offer for these sorts of questions. He extends this confrontation away from the purely abstract and textual, providing it a real-world impact when he suggests that *A History of Violence* 'forces us to confront our Pavlovian conditioning to violence, whether we are watching real military campaigns with living room detachment or whooping and hollering for fictional ones.'[42] Similarly, for *Rolling Stone*'s Peter Travers the film offers 'a study of how we wrap our Jones for violence in God, country, family and any other excuse that's handy. You know the drill. So does George Bush.'[43] And for Amy Taubin, who selected the film as the best of 2005 in *Art Forum*, 'the insanity is institutional, implicating us all.'[44] In short, these critics see in Cronenberg's film some sort of indictment of American society as a whole, each agreeing that the film is saying *something* about the important issues that it raises, even if the conclusions drawn are somewhat vague.

Certainly, the statement by Cronenberg about the 'interbleeding of genre, myth and realpolitik,' with which I opened this chapter, signals a certain political disposition that accords well with the readings offered by these various critics. In discussing the film with the press, the director maintains that the film

> does have political undertones, or overtones, although it's not overtly political. Those are things that Viggo and I discussed a lot when I was trying to convince him to do the movie. You have a man who's defending his family and his home against bad guys with guns. It raises the question of retribution. Is anything justified when you're attacked? It's also hard not to notice that George Bush uses American Western movies as a model for his foreign policy – Osama bin Laden wanted dead or alive.[45]

Cronenberg's willingness to accord the film political overtones is something of a radical departure from past statements about his films, in which he has demonstrated disdain for political filmmakers. Significantly, in his interview with Serge Grünberg conducted after the

Cannes screening of *A History of Violence* but published only after its release, Cronenberg said of the film:

> I think that politics has no place in art, because you lose the subtlety. And when you lose the subtlety, you are losing the human reality, because it is very subtle and complex, and I can see that in politics you maybe at times cannot afford to be bogged down, because you would be forced into action if you had to address every complexity. But this is art, you know, and this isn't propaganda, this isn't a political statement, this is an artistic statement.[46]

How can we reconcile these very different statements? One way would be to assume that David Cronenberg, an 'apolitical' filmmaker who, as Peter Morris has pointed out, once seemed deeply in accord with William S. Burroughs's suggestion that political change was pointless, as it merely substituted one system for another,[47] in his sixties has reversed his earlier sentiments and turned to a form of political engagement with his work. This is the approach taken by many American critics, who see in *A History of Violence* a specific critique of the Bush administration's international policies. Yet if we choose to believe that Cronenberg is speaking honestly to Grünberg, it would seem that the other possibility is that the film is not truly political in the sense that the critics are making it out to be, but is merely masquerading as a critique of American culture. Cronenberg himself has emphasized the way that critics tend to misread his work because they are focused largely on the present: 'reviewers are very plugged in to what's happening now. The connections they tend to make are of the moment.'[48] Following this logic, it is possible to see Cronenberg as a filmmaker who is masquerading as political, who is providing critics with a story upon which they can project their own political interests without an actual commitment from the director himself. In this way, Cronenberg adopts another mask, one that allows his film to pass as something that it might not be, much as Joey passes for so long as Tom. If this is the case, the question remains: is there a truth to this film behind its various forms of masquerade?

To answer that question it might be worth considering one final act of masquerade presented by *A History of Violence*: the way that Canada stands in for the United States. Critics have unanimously agreed that Millbrook does not seem in any way to be a real American town. Not unlike David Lynch's Lumberton, North Carolina, in *Blue Velvet*, Millbrook is the America of 'Norman Rockwell and Quaker Oats commercials,'[49] featuring 'a pair of cartoonishly good-looking normals, living with their CGI-perfect children'[50] in 'a Capra picture, perhaps, with Viggo Mortensen as Jimmy Stewart.'[51] The false sense of America created by location shooting in Canada has been a Cronenberg hallmark for some time. In an interview with Anne Billson, he suggests that this displacement makes his work more eerily dreamlike: 'The streets look American, but they're not, and the accents are American, but not quite. Everything's a little off-kilter; it's sort of like a dream image of America.'[52] In *A History of Violence*, it is not entirely clear that Cronenberg is even at great pains to mask the substitution of Canada for the United States. Pointedly, when Joey drives from Millbrook to Philadelphia on his way to confront Richie, the montage includes a highway sign with the speed limit posted as 90 km per hour. Of all the second-unit footage shot for the film, it is difficult to imagine that the road sign appeared in the finished movie simply through a lack of attention to detail. Indeed, it is perhaps easier to believe that, like Tom when he kills Leland, there is a part of Cronenberg that wants to be found out, that toys with this mask in the hope that his true identity will be freed to rise to the surface.

Conclusion

I don't have a moral plan. I'm a Canadian.

David Cronenberg[1]

If David Cronenberg, like Joey Cusack, is a masked man in *A History of Violence*, the identity that he is hiding is that of a distinctly Canadian filmmaker who nonetheless makes films that explore the frayed edges of American cinematic traditions. Cronenberg's Canadian-ness has long troubled scholars and critics. Few Canadian filmmakers have spent more time working outside the country, or in genres that are so atypical of Canadian production history. William Beard, in a 1994 essay entitled 'The Canadianness of David Cronenberg,' suggests that it is the director's reliance on popular genres that separates his work from 'the depressive English-Canadian cinema they might otherwise clearly resemble.'[2] He suggests that the 'thematic dualism' of Cronenberg's cinema is matched by a 'dualism of articulation' that equates repression with a Canadian subject position and unrepression with an American one.[2] From this point of view it is possible to argue, as Beard does, that the hero of *The Dead Zone*, a film whose action is unambiguously set in the United States, is 'the most "Canadian" of all Cronenberg's post-*Scanners* protagonists.'[3] This dualistic view is somewhat at odds with Geoff

Pevere's suggestion that Cronenberg's male leads problematize the standard conception of Canadian-ness as acquiescent and pensive. He suggests that Cronenberg views the 'accommodating, thoughtful Canadian exterior [as] a veneer that has been maintained only at the cost of a great and ever-increasing repression of psychosexual impulses.'[4] That this description, published almost a quarter-century before Cronenberg brought Tom Stall to life on screen, is uncannily accurate in describing *A History of Violence* goes almost without saying. If the classic model of the masculine masquerade proposed by Joan Riviere implies a process of feminization, this film suggests that it might more appropriately be thought of as a Canadianization, which, of course, might be only a different term for feminization. In other words, the feminization of Tom isn't as much a commentary on sexuality and gender roles within the family as a larger exploration of geopolitical relations across national borders and the kinds of cultural tropes that they engender in their cinema.

As if to give credence to that suggestion, Cronenberg argues in an interview in the Canadian news magazine *Maclean's* that the film is neither Canadian nor American, but a hybrid: 'if we're talking creative categories, it's a true Canada-U.S. co-production.'[5] Piers Handling, whose essay 'A Canadian Cronenberg' situates the director within the traditions of Canadian filmmaking, notes the way that the director's films are looked upon as 'aberrations in the cinematic landscape of this country: stylistically and imaginatively the films apparently do not belong.'[6] Handling sees a tremendous distance between Cronenberg's populist and fantastic overtones and the realist and documentary traditions that have long characterized film production in Canada. Of course, by 2005 the realist and documentary traditions of Canadian filmmaking were little more than an imagined heritage, a remnant of a stereotyped image of Canada as the producer of an art-oriented 'cinema we need' in opposition to the crassly mercantile 'cinema of greed' produced by Hollywood. *A History of Violence*, which slyly crosses postmodern affectations and art cinema ambiguity with a blood-drenched meditation on American mythologies, exploits, more than most films, the tension that exists between the vulgar self-stereotypes of both Canadian and American cinemas. The ironic distance that is built into his portrait of American life, what Manohla Dargis calls 'an America that bears little relation to the real thing and looks a lot like the fabricated country familiar from countless Hollywood movies,'[7] alerts us to the presence of a mask, to the fact that this is not a film about the United States, but only one that is pretending to be.

Dargis argues in the *New York Times*, 'Mr. Cronenberg, a Canadian, is taking aim at this country, to be sure.'[8] But like everything else in this film, nothing is really sure. If we step back from *A History of Violence*, it looks a lot less like a film about America and a lot more like a film about American cinema. But if we take one further step back, a different image comes into focus. This is not simply a film *about* a man who is masquerading as a respectable midwestern family man, repressing his violent heritage to live the life he wants. This is a film *by* a man who is masquerading as a respectable American commercial filmmaker, repressing his violent heritage to make the film that he wants. And what is being masked other than his Canadian identity? As Brian Johnson suggests, 'Tom could be Cronenberg himself: a nice guy living in a small town called Canada, minding the saloon, or salon, of art-house cinema. Men in black, the Hollywood suits, ask him to show his stuff, to direct some gunplay. And he delivers.'[9] Of course, he has also delivered much more than mere gunplay, suffusing his film with traces of his Canadian identity. To this end, it seems not so much a commentary on America, or on American film violence as it is a reflection on a specifically Canadian detachedness about its relationship to the United States.

Writing in the *New Yorker*, David Denby suggests that *A History of Violence* 'asks us to believe that one man can carry two entirely different personalities within him and still be as sane as daylight.'[11] To my mind, this does not accurately describe the Tom/Joey relationship as much as it might describe the mindset of a filmmaker who is seeking to make sense of the history of American cinematic violence from a Canadian perspective, a task that is liable to drive anyone crazy. Throughout the film, Cronenberg proves himself to be a historian of violence, relentlessly categorizing and citing endless variations of cinematic inhumanity. More important, he does it all while masking his own signature as a filmmaker known for his explicit and controversial violent imagery. Christine Ramsay has insightfully argued, 'Cronenberg repeatedly draws parallels between himself and his heroes, as if, indeed, they are his "persona" in his films.'[11] This seems to be the case in A History of Violence as well, as the director ably mimics his lead character, pretending to be the cinephile that he is not while allowing subtle instances of the 'real' Cronenberg to shine through on occasion. Yet the question necessarily arises: if Cronenberg has constructed his film in such a way that his own role is a mirror of Joey's, where does that leave the audience, who have been deceived by this masquerade?

It seems that the viewer is perhaps in a position akin to that of Edie, the supportive wife who assumed that things were as they appeared to be, but who has now, to her horror, discovered otherwise. Manohla Dargis's previously cited suggestion that Edie is transformed in the film into 'a gangster's moll with a taste for a little rough trade'[12] seems to oversimplify the Stalls' relationship by situating it too deeply within the single cinematic context of film noir. If Edie is a femme fatale, she is a remarkably, and atypically, guilt-ridden one, far removed from the likes of Kitty Collins (Ava Gardner) in The Killers, begging her dying husband to 'lie his soul into hell.' It is significant that, after the violent sex scene on the stairs, Edie never again speaks. It was a Canadian critic, Rick Groen, writing in the Globe and Mail, who notably highlighted the combination of 'intense excitement and residual guilt' that is aroused by

4.1. Edie finally sees the truth. ©MMV, New Line Productions, Inc.
All rights reserved. Photo by Takashi Seida. Photo appears courtesy of
New Line Productions, Inc.

the combination of sex and violence in this scene.[13] This combination of sex and guilt is something that Katherine Monk argues is a significant trope in Canadian cinema because 'sex = guilt in Canadian society, no matter which way you undress it.'[14] If what Monk terms 'weird sex' troubles both Canada and Edie Stall, then it seems appropriate to imply a parallel between the two. Further, if, as Brian Johnson remarks in *Maclean's*, Tom Stall is 'a mild-mannered family man so quiet and unassuming he could be Canadian,'[15] it might be equally plausible to suggest that Edie Stall is so trusting and loyal that she might be Canadian as well.

Does this mean that, following Dargis, Canadian audiences similarly have a secret desire to be treated roughly by their cinema? Given the relative successes of American genre films and what Beard terms 'the Canadian drama of restraint' at the Canadian box office,[16] it would be difficult to suggest that these longings are particularly secret. It might be more accurate to ask, therefore, whether, like Edie, Canadians feel guilty about acting on these desires? Should Canadians feel dirty when filmmakers like David Cronenberg give us the type of films that we want? Moreover, has the resulting guilt about having those desires met rendered us increasingly unable to give voice to the Canadian imagination? As early as 1994 Beard argued that in Cronenberg's cinema 'the Canadian drama of restraint, internalized violence and stasis, and the American drama of freedom, externalized violence and progress, have their equivalents in the frozen despairing inner identity and explosive visceral outer genre-qualities of the films.'[17] Largely lacking indigenous myths of aggression, it is perhaps not surprising that a Canadian filmmaker turns his eye towards America to mine an archive of cinematic violence. These are not Canadian stories that Cronenberg is working through in *A History of Violence*, but they speak acutely to Canadian audiences nonetheless.

At the risk of generalizing a Canadian experience, I nonetheless want to suggest that there is something specific to this most American of Cronenberg's films that highlights Canadian filmmaking and film-viewing practices. Canadians often draw distinctions between them-selves and the cultural behemoth to south, while simultaneously deriv-ing pleasure from its domination. Like Edie, they are wracked with guilt by their awareness that what they want is not what they think might be best, and so they sit passively, even sullenly, across the table from the enemy that they desire. In that sense, then, *A History of Violence* may seem at first to be a history of American cinematic violence, a story – to use William Hurt's Latinized translation – of an American culture that is almost too easy to critique. However, I want to suggest that such a read-ing ultimately masks a deeper, more pernicious story about Canada's visceral relationship to American culture and its desire to consume even as it is consumed by it. The last words Edie speaks in *A History of Vio-lence* may be the defiant 'Fuck you, Joey!' but it is she who pulls him into her erotic embrace.

Production Credits

Director
David Cronenberg

Writers
John Wagner and Vince Locke (graphic novel)
Josh Olson (screenplay)

Cast

Viggo Mortensen	Tom Stall
Maria Bello	Edie Stall
Ed Harris	Carl Fogarty
William Hurt	Richie Cusack
Ashton Holmes	Jack Stall
Peter MacNeill	Sheriff Sam Carney
Stephen McHattie	Leland
Greg Bryk	Billy
Kyle Schmid	Bobby
Sumela Kay	Judy Danvers
Gerry Quigley	Mick
Deborah Drakeford	Charlotte
Heidi Hayes	Sarah Stall
Aidan Devine	Charlie Roarke
Bill MacDonald	Frank Mulligan
Michelle McCree	Jenny Wyeth

Ian Matthews	Ruben
R.D. Reid	Pat
Morgan Kelly	Bobby's Buddy
Martha Reilly	Shoe Saleswoman
Jason Barbeck	Richie's Thug
Bruce Beaton	Richie's Thug
Neven Pajkic	Richie's Thug
Brendan Connor	Local TV Reporter
Nick Antonacci	Local TV Reporter
John Watson	Baseball Coach
Don Allison	TV Broadcaster
Brittany Payer	Motel Girl
Mitch Boughs	Kid in Diner
April Mullen	Kid in Diner
George King	Hospital Well-Wisher
Shawn Campbell	Orderly

Producers
Kent Alterman (executive producer)
Chris Bender (producer)
Cale Boyter (executive producer)
Josh Braun (executive producer)
Toby Emmerich (executive producer)
Justis Greene (executive producer)
Roger E. Kass (executive producer)
J.C. Spink (producer)
Jake Weiner (co-producer)

Original Music
Howard Shore

Director of Photography
Peter Suschitzky

Film Editor
Ronald Sanders

Casting
Deirdre Bowen
Mark Bennett (USA)

Production Design
Carol Spier

Art Direction
James McAteer

Set Decoration
Peter P. Nicolakakos

Costume Design
Denise Cronenberg

Makeup Department
Stéphan Dupuis (makeup supervisor)

Assistant Director
Walter Gasparovic (first assistant director)
Robert Warwick (second assistant director)

Sound Department
Jennifer Dunnington (music editor)
Wayne Griffin (supervising sound editor)
Michael O'Farrell (supervising sound editor)

Special Effects
Neil Trifunovich (special effects supervisor)

Runtime
96 minutes

Aspect Ratio
1.85 : 1

Further Viewing

Cape Fear. J. Lee Thompson. Universal Pictures, 1962
The Killers. Robert Siodmak. Universal Pictures, 1946
Out of the Past. Jacques Tourner. RKO Radio Pictures, 1947
Point Blank. John Boorman. Metro-Goldwyn-Mayer, 1967
Shane. George Stevens. Paramount Pictures, 1943
The Wrong Man. Alfred Hitchcock. Warner Brothers Pictures, 1956

Notes

1. Introduction

1 William Beard and Piers Handling, 'The Interview,' in *The Shape of Rage: The Films of David Cronenberg*, ed. Piers Handling (Toronto: General, 1983), 195.

2 J. Hoberman, 'Violent Reaction,' *Village Voice*, 29 December 2005. Available at http://www.villagevoice.com/take/seven.php?page=hoberman

3 Manohla Dargis, 'Once Disaster Hits, It Seems Never to End,' *New York Times*, 23 September 2005, E1.

4 Desson Thomson, 'The Likable Face of "Violence,"' *Washington Post*, 23 September 2005, C04.

5 Kenneth Turan, 'A History of Violence,' *Los Angeles Times*, 23 September 2005. Available at http://www.calendarlive.com/movies/turan/cl-et-violence 23sep23,0,1300476.story

6 J. Hoberman, 'Historical Oversight,' *Village Voice*, 24 May 2005. Available at http://www.villagevoice.com/film/0521,hoberman1,64285,20.html.

7 Rene Rodriguez, 'In "History," Violence Is Just a Part of Our Human Nature,' *Miami Herald*, 30 September 2005. Available at http://ae.miami.com/entertainment/ui/miami/movie.html?id=425 572&reviewId=19149

8 Scott Foundas, 'Don't Tread on Me,' *LA Weekly*, 15 September 2005. Available at http://www.laweekly.com/film+tv/film/dont-tread-on-me/277/

9 Rodriguez, 'In "History."'

10 *A History of Violence Digital Press Kit* (Los Angeles: New Line Cinema, 2005), 15.

11 David Edelstein, 'Art for Arteries' Sake,' *Slate* 23, September 2005. Available at http://www.slate.com/id/2126742/?nav=fo

12 William Beard, 'The Canadianness of David Cronenberg,' *Mosaic* 27:2 (1994): 115.

13 Claudia Springer, 'The Seduction of the Surface: From Alice to Crash,' *Feminist Media Studies* 1:2 (2001): 12.

14 Christine Ramsay, 'Dead Queers: One Legacy of the Trope of "Mind Over Matter" in the Films of David Cronenberg,' *Canadian Journal of Film Studies* 8:1 (1999): 53.

15 Robin Wood, 'Cronenberg: A Dissenting View,' in *The Shape of Rage: The Films of David Cronenberg*, ed. Piers Handling (Toronto: General, 1983), 131.

16 Chris Rodley, *Cronenberg on Cronenberg* (London: Faber & Faber, 1992), 68.

17 Allison Benedikt, 'A History of Violence,' *Chicago Tribune*, 23 September 2005. Available at http://metromix.chicagotribune.com/movies/mmx-050923-movies-review-history,0,1239765.story?coll=mmx-movies_top_heds

18 Turan 'A History of Violence.'

19 Beard, 'Canadianness of David Cronenberg,' 117.

20 William Beard, *The Artist as Monster: The Cinema of David Cronenberg* (Toronto: University of Toronto Press, 2006), 66.

21 Brian D. Johnson, 'Violence Hits Home,' *Maclean's*, 17 October 2005, 48.

2. A History

1 Steven Frank, 'Inside the Mind of Cronenberg,' *Time* [Canadian edition], 19 September 2005, 48.

2 Wood, 'Cronenberg,' 115.

3 Beard, *Artist as Monster*, 342.

4 Denis Seguin, 'The Screen Machine,' *Canadian Business* 29 (August 2005): 36.

5 *A History of Violence* Movie, 'Q + A.' Available at www.historyofviolence.com

6 *A History of Violence Digital Press Kit*, 5.

7 Ibid., 9–10.

8 Richard Corliss, 'Inner Truths,' *Time* [Canadian edition], 19 September 2005, 50.

9 *A History of Violence Digital Press Kit* 11.

10 Ibid., 13, 14.

11 *A History of Violence* Movie

12 Rebecca Murray, interview with *A History of Violence* director David Cronenberg. Available at *About.com.* (http://movies.about.com/od/ahistoryofviolence/a/violence072 605.htm)

13 Mark Browning, *David Cronenberg: Author or Film-Maker?* (London: Intellect Books, 2007) 8.

14 Murray, Interview.

15 Jeffrey Sconce, 'Irony, Nihilism, and the American 'Smart' Film,' *Screen* 43:3 (2003).

16 John Wagner and Vince Locke, *A History of Violence* (New York: Vertigo Books, 2005) 187.

3. Violence

1 Amy Taubin, 'Model Citizens,' *Film Comment* (September-October 2005): 24.

2 Serge Grünberg, *David Cronenberg* (London: Plexus, 2006), 4.

3 Wagner and Locke, *A History of Violence*, 11–13.

4 Ramsay, 'Dead Queers,' 45–62.

5 Thomas Waugh, *The Romance of Transgression in Canada: Queering Sexualities, Nations, Cinemas* (Montreal: McGill-Queen's University Press), 397.

6 Lee Horsley, 'The Development of Post-War Literary and Cinematic Noir,' *Crime Culture*, 2002. Available at (http://www.crimeculture.com/Contents/Film%20Noir.html).

7 Robert B. Ray, *A Certain Tendency of Hollywood Cinema, 1930–1980* (Princeton, NJ: Princeton University Press, 1985), 145.

8 Richard Corliss, 'Sticking to Their Guns,' *Time*, 26 September 2005. Available at http://www.time.com/time/magazine/article/0,9171,1106325-2,0 0.html

9 Dargis, 'Once Disaster Hits,' E1.

10 Stuart Klawans, 'Lessons of Darkness,' *The Nation*, 24 October 2005, 48.

11 Ken Tucker, 'View to a Chill,' *New York*. Available at http://nymag.com/nymetro/movies/reviews/14698/

12 Richard Alleva, 'Public Enemy,' *Commonweal*, 21 October 2005, 25.

13 Peter Travers, 'King Clooney and the 10 Best Movies of 2005,' *Rolling Stone*, 16

December 2005. Available at http://www.rollingstone.com/news/story/8952409/king_clooney_ and_the_10_best_movies_of_2005

14 Graham Fuller, 'Good Guy, Bad Guy,' *Sight and Sound*, October 2005, 16, 14.

15 Ibid., 14.

16 Jonathan Rosenbaum, 'A Depth in The Family,' *The Chicago Reader* 5 Sept. 2005. Available at http://www.chicagoreader.com/movies/archives/2005/0905/05093 0.html

17 William Beard, 'The Visceral Mind: The Major Films of David Cronenberg,' in *The Shape of Rage: The Films of David Cronenberg*, ed. Piers Handling (Toronto: General, 1983), 1.

18 Peter Morris, *David Cronenberg: A Delicate Balance* (Toronto: ECW Press, 1994), 10.

19 Beard, *Artist as Monster*, 113.

20 Ibid., 76, 167, 247, 354.

21 Morris, *David Cronenberg*, 102.

22 Chris Rodley, *Cronenberg on Cronenberg* (London: Faber & Faber, 1992), 82.

23 Barbara Creed, 'The Naked Crunch: Cronenberg's Homoerotic Bodies,' in *The Modern Fantastic: The Films of David Cronenberg*, ed. Michael Grant (Trowbridge, U.K.: Flicks Books, 2000), 84.

24 Beard, *Artist as Monster*, 66.

25 John Harkness, 'The Word, The Flesh and David Cronenberg,' in *The Shape of Rage: The Films of David Cronenberg*, ed. Piers Handling (Toronto: General, 1983), 90.

26 Beard, *Artist as Monster*, 11.

27 Robin Wood, 'An Introduction to the American Horror Film,' in *Movies and Methods*. Volume II: *An Anthology*, ed. Bill Nichols (Los Angeles: University of California Press, 1985), 216–17.

28 Ridley, *Cronenberg*, 65.

29 Katherine Monk, *Weird Sex and Snowshoes and Other Canadian Film Phenomena* (Vancouver: Raincoast Books, 2001), 143.

30 Manohla Dargis, 'Dark Truths of a Killing Love,' *New York Times*, 15 January 2006, 2A1.

31 Robert S. Miller, 'A History of Violence: Search for Meaninglessness,' *Arctic*

Shores Contemporary Reviews. Available at http://catharticreviews.spaces.live
.com/blog/cns!48920781E15 60168!405.entry

32 Murray, Interview.

33 Monk, *Weird Sex*, 236.

34 Dargis, 'Dark Truths,' 2A1.

35 Ibid.

36 Grünberg, *David Cronenberg*, 173.

37 Richard Stayton, 'Rough Sex Education,' *Written By.* February-March 2006.
Available at http://www.wga.org/writtenby/writtenbysub.aspx?id=1635

38 Ibid.

39 Joan Riviere, 'Womanliness as Masquerade,' in *Formations of Fantasy*, ed. Victor Burgin, James Donald, and Cora Kaplan (New York: Methuen, 1986), 38.

40 Harry Brod, 'Masculinity as Masquerade,' in *The Masculine Masquerade: Masculinity and Representation*, ed. Andrew Perchuk and Helaine Posner (Cambridge, MA: MIT Press, 1995) 17.

41 Steven Cohan, 'The Spy in the Gray Flannel Suit: Gender Performance and the Representation of Masculinity,' in *The Masculine Masquerade: Masculinity and Representation*, ed. Andrew Perchuk and Helaine Posner (Cambridge, MA: MIT Press, 1995), 44.

42 Thomson, 'Likable Face,' C04.

43 Peter Travers 'History of Violence,' *Rolling Stone*, 22 September 2005. Available at http://www.rollingstone.com/reviews/movie/6824681/history_of
_violence

44 Amy Taubin, 'Film: Best of 2005,' *Artforum International*, December 2005, 54.

45 Johnson, 'Violence Hits Home,' 49.

46 Grünberg, *David Cronenberg*, 174.

47 Morris, *David Cronenberg*, 27.

48 Chris Ridley, *Cronenberg*, 128.

49 Scott Foundas, 'Don't Tread on Me.'

50 Hoberman, 'Historical Oversight.'

51 Roger Ebert. 'A History of Violence,' *Chicago Sun-Times*, 23 September 2005.
Available at http://rogerebert.suntimes.com/apps/pbcs.dll/article?AID=/
20050922/REVIEWS/50919002/1023

52 Quoted in Morris, *David Cronenberg*, 106.

4. Conclusion

1 Geoff Pevere, 'Cronenberg Tackles Dominant Videology,' in *The Shape of Rage: The Films of David Cronenberg*, ed. Piers Handling (Toronto: General, 1983) 141.

2 Beard, 'Canadianness of David Cronenberg,' 128, 129.

3 Beard, *Artist as Monster*, 192.

4 Pevere, 'Cronenberg Tackles Dominant Videology,' 141.

5 Johnson, 'Violence Hits Home,' 49.

6 Piers Handling, 'A Canadian Cronenberg,' in *The Shape of Rage: The Films of David Cronenberg*, ed. Piers Handling (Toronto: General, 1983) 98.

7 Manohla Dargis, Revisiting the Past by Way of Cannes,' *New York Times*, 20 May 2005, E1.

8 Dargis, 'Once Disaster Hits,' E1.

9 Brian D. Johnson, 'Crapshoot at Cannes,' *Maclean's*, 30 May 2005, ??.

10 David Denby, 'A History of Violence,' *New Yorker*, 7 November 2005, 28.

11 Ramsay, 'Dead Queers,' 52.

12 Dargis, 'Dark Truths,' 2A1.

13 Rick Groen, 'Dissecting the Monster Within,' *Globe and Mail*, 23 September 2005, R5.

14 Monk, *Weird Sex*, 120.

15 Johnson, 'Violence Hits Home,' 48.

16 Beard 'Canadianness of David Cronenberg,' 129.

17 Ibid.

Selected Bibliography

Original Graphic Novel

Wagner, John and Vince Locke. *A History of Violence*. New York: Vertigo Books, 2005

On David Cronenberg

Beard, William. 'The Canadianness of David Cronenberg.' *Mosaic* 27 (June 1994): 113–33.
– *The Artist as Monster: The Cinema of David Cronenberg*. Toronto: University of Toronto Press, 2006.
Grant, Michael (ed.). *The Modern Fantastic: The Films of David Cronenberg*. Trowbridge: Flicks Books, 2004.
Grünberg, Serge. *David Cronenberg*. London: Plexus, 2006.
Handling, Piers (ed.). *The Shape of Rage: The Films of David Cronenberg*. Toronto: General Publishing, 1983.
Morris, Peter. *David Cronenberg: A Delicate Balance*. Toronto: ECW Press, 1994.
Rodley, Chris. *Cronenberg on Cronenberg*. London: Faber and Faber, 1992.

Masculinity and Masquerade

Beaver, Harold. *The Great American Masquerade*. London: Vision Press, 1985.
Perchuk, Andrew, and Helaine Posner (eds.). *The Masculine Masquerade: Masculinity and Representation*. Cambridge: MIT Visual Arts Center, 1995.

Reviews of *A History of Violence*

Dargis, Manohla. 'Dark Truths of a Killing Love.' *New York Times*, 15 January 2006, 2A1.

Fuller, Graham. 'Good Guy Bad Guy.' *Sight and Sound*, 15 (October 2005), 12–16.

Johnson, Brian D. 'Violence Hits Home.' *Maclean's*, 17 October 2005, 48–9.

Klawans, Stuart. 'Lessons of Darkness.' *The Nation*, 24 October 2005, 48–52.

Taubin, Amy. 'Model Citizens.' *Film Comment* (September-October 2005): 24–8.

CANADIAN CINEMA

Edited by Bart Beaty and Will Straw